THE 2010 BOOK OF
AVIATION WONDER

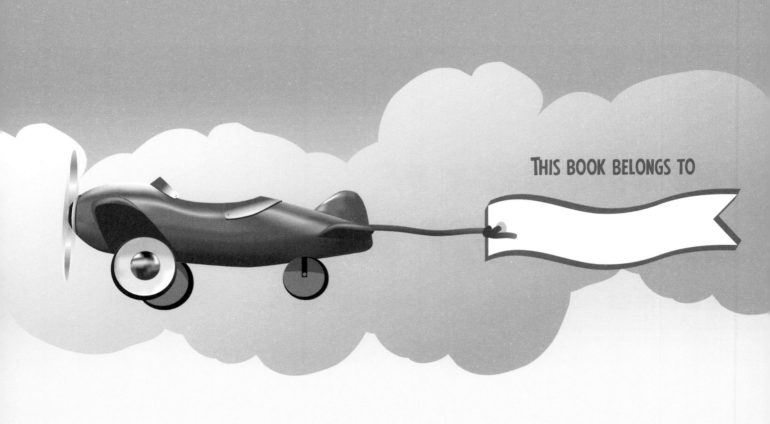

THIS BOOK BELONGS TO

THE 2010 BOOK OF
AVIATION WONDER
CELEBRATING FLIGHT SINCE 1910

Bristol Cultural Development Partnership

Published by:
Bristol Cultural Development Partnership (BCDP)
Leigh Court, Abbots Leigh, Bristol BS8 3RA

Design and typesetting by Qube Design Associates Ltd
Printed in England by Butler Tanner & Dennis Ltd

2010

ISBN 978 0 9550742 4 0

© BCDP

We are grateful for the support of the Heritage Lottery Fund, which has
kindly funded this publication:

A project of Bristol Cultural Development Partnership
(trading as Bristol Creative Projects):

The 2010 Book of Aviation Wonder is published as part of the BAC
100 celebrations marking the centenary of the founding of the Bristol
Aeroplane Company. For more information, please visit the website:
www.bac2010.co.uk

Home of the British Aviation Industry

We would like to thank all those who have provided illustrative
material for this book. They are credited by each image. No image
in this book should be reproduced without first ascertaining who
holds the reproduction rights and getting the appropriate permission.
Advertisement for men's fashion on page 16 given to the Victoria &
Albert Museum by H. L. Sparks, Esq. Poster of Charlie Chaplin on
page 17 given to the Victoria & Albert Museum by Jordison & Co Ltd,
copyright Bubbles Incorporated SA 1997.

CONTENTS

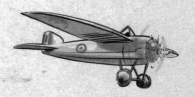

Dear Reader

If you like aeroplanes - watching them, flying in them, making paper ones, pretending to <u>be</u> one - 2010 is an exciting year for you.

You can join thousands of people who are celebrating the centenary of the founding of the Bristol Aeroplane Company, also known as 'the BAC'. A centenary is a hundred years and to found something is to start it so this is a great big 100th birthday bash for the BAC.

If there hadn't been the Bristol Aeroplane Company then we wouldn't have had the Bristol Boxkite, the Bristol Fighter, the Blenheim, Britannia, Concorde, the Airbus A380 and lots of other aircraft. We also wouldn't have had some very important engines like the Jupiter, Centaurus, Proteus, Pegasus and Olympus.

In the early days, 'Bristol' aeroplanes were built by the British & Colonial Aeroplane Company which had been founded on the same day in 1910 as the BAC. It was also founded by the same man - Sir George White. Later on other company names were used and new companies were founded. It's a complicated story but we'll try to keep it simple and just concentrate on some of the wonderful things that been made in and around Bristol and South Gloucestershire by the local aviation industry. And that's not just aeroplanes and engines, but also boats, buildings, comet interceptors and cars.

In this book you can find out about how aeroplanes fly, what wings and propellers do, how piston and jet engines work, and how the Harrier is able to 'jump'. You can also find out how BAC is connected to Charles Rolls who was killed in an aeroplane crash the same year that the company was founded. There are activities taking place in Monmouth, his home town, in 2010 to celebrate his life and work.

On these pages there are puzzles, things to do, comic strips, fascinating facts, history and science, a look into the future, stories about famous people, and lots and lots of pictures.

So join in the fun in 2010 and enjoy this special Book of Aviation Wonder.

From The Book of Aviation Wonder Team

SIR GEORGE WHITE
THE BOXKITE BARONET

GEORGE WHITE WAS A BRILLIANT BUSINESSMAN WHOSE MANY ACHIEVEMENTS MADE BRISTOL FAMOUS AROUND THE WORLD. THE CITY AND SURROUNDING AREA HAVE BEEN AN IMPORTANT HOME OF AIRCRAFT AND AERO ENGINES EVER SINCE HE SET UP HIS AEROPLANE COMPANY IN 1910.

DURING THE FIRST WORLD WAR THOUSANDS OF BRISTOL-MADE AIRCRAFT TOOK TO THE SKIES, MAKING THE SOLDIERS BELOW A LITTLE SAFER.

AND DOWN IN THE TRENCHES, ONE SOLDIER HAD EVEN MORE REASON TO THANK GEORGE WHITE.

LOOK OUT!

AARGH!

IS... IS HE DEAD?

I'M NOT DEAD, YOU IDIOT. LOOK!

THE COIN SIR GEORGE GAVE ME.

TALK ABOUT LUCKY!

GEORGE NEVER FORGOT HIS OLD SCHOOL, ST. MICHAEL'S, BRISTOL, AND EVERY YEAR HE PRESENTED A SPECIAL COIN AS A PRIZE.

MONEY IS OFTEN MENTIONED IN THE STORY OF GEORGE WHITE. HE MADE A LOT OF MONEY AND HE OFTEN USED IT TO MAKE LIFE BETTER FOR PEOPLE.

BUT AS WE WILL SEE, HE HIMSELF STARTED OUT WITH VERY LITTLE...

GEORGE'S FATHER HENRY WORKED AS A PAINTER AND DECORATOR AND HIS MOTHER ELIZA WAS IN SERVICE AS A LADY'S MAID.

THEY MARRIED IN 1843 AND MOVED TO NO.2 ST. MICHAEL'S BUILDINGS, IN KINGSDOWN, BRISTOL. GEORGE WAS THEIR FOURTH CHILD, BORN ON 28 MARCH 1854.

AT ST. MICHAEL'S BOYS' SCHOOL, GEORGE WAS A BRIGHT AND HARDWORKING STUDENT. HE LEFT AT 15 AND BECAME A CLERK AT STANLEY & WASBROUGH A BIG LAW FIRM IN CORN ST.

YOU'RE DOING JOLLY WELL, YOUNG WHITE. WE'D LIKE *YOU* TO ARRANGE THE *TRAM SYNDICATE*.

THE *TRAM* WAS A NEW FORM OF TRANSPORT IN BRISTOL AT THE TIME, FASTER AND CHEAPER THAN THE OLD OMNIBUSES. GEORGE WAS GIVEN THE JOB OF TAKING LEGAL CONTROL OF THE COUNCIL'S TRAM LINE.

AT ONLY 20, HE SO IMPRESSED THE NEW BRISTOL TRAMWAY COMPANY THEY MADE HIM THEIR COMPANY SECRETARY. HE ALSO JOINED BRISTOL'S STOCK EXCHANGE AND BEGAN MAKING A LOT OF MONEY.

SOON A NETWORK OF TRAMLINES MOVED PEOPLE COMFORTABLY AROUND BRISTOL.

ALTHOUGH NOT IN THE WEALTHY SUBURB OF CLIFTON!

To
The Editor
Bristol Mercury
Sir
Is it not something terrible and most wicked that the disgusting tramway is to bring the nasty, low inhabitants of Bristol up into our sacred region? We have nothing common or unclean amongst us at present. Poor people do not walk about on Clifton streets... they should stay in their homes.

GEORGE WAS VERY *BUSY*, INVESTING IN RAILWAYS AND OTHER TRANSPORT SCHEMES. BUT HE FOUND TIME TO MARRY CAROLINE ROSINA THOMAS IN 1876.

IN 1895 HIS STANDING IN THE BUSINESS COMMUNITY GREW WHEN HE OPENED BRITAIN'S FIRST *ELECTRIC* TRAM SERVICE IN BRISTOL. CHEAPER AND MORE POWERFUL THAN THE HORSE-DRAWN TRAMS, THE NEW KINGSWOOD - ST. GEORGE LINE WAS A GREAT SUCCESS.

AS GEORGE BECAME *RICHER*, HE BECAME MORE INVOLVED IN CHARITABLE WORK. HE ORGANISED A BIG CARNIVAL AT BRISTOL ZOO TO HELP *BRISTOL ROYAL INFIRMARY* WHICH WAS HEAVILY IN DEBT, AND HE SPENT THOUSANDS OF POUNDS OF HIS OWN MONEY TO HELP BUILD A NEW EXTENSION TO THE HOSPITAL.

HE SET UP A BRANCH OF THE *RED CROSS* CHARITY IN BRISTOL, AND DONATED AND FUND-RAISED FOR MANY CAUSES. HE WAS REWARDED FOR HIS EFFORTS IN 1904 WHEN HE WAS MADE A *BARONET*, BY THE KING.

SIR GEORGE, AS HE WAS NOW KNOWN, WAS INTERESTED IN ALL KINDS OF TRANSPORT, NOT JUST TRAMS AND RAILWAYS. HE OWNED SEVERAL CARS AND INTRODUCED MOTOR BUSES AND MOTOR TAXIS TO BRISTOL. BUT IT WAS STILL A SHOCK TO THE OTHER BRISTOL TRAMWAYS SHAREHOLDERS WHEN IN 1910 HE ANNOUNCED HIS NEWEST INTEREST...

AVIATION?

THE SUBJECT SEEMS TO OFFER PROMISE OF *DEVELOPMENT*... MY BROTHER AND I HAVE DETERMINED *PERSONALLY* TO TAKE THE RISKS AND EXPENSE OF THE ENDEAVOUR TO DEVELOP THE SCIENCE FROM THE *SPECTACULAR* AND *COMMERCIAL* OR *MANUFACTURING* POINT OF VIEW.

BECAUSE HIS HEALTH WAS GETTING WORSE, GEORGE OFTEN MADE TRIPS TO SOUTHERN FRANCE AND IT WAS THERE THAT HE FIRST SAW BIPLANES. HE EVEN SAW WILBUR WRIGHT FLYING.

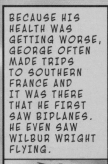

IN FEBRUARY 1910, HE FOUNDED 'THE BRITISH & COLONIAL AEROPLANE COMPANY' WITH HIS BROTHER SAMUEL, HIS SON GEORGE STANLEY AND TWO OF HIS NEPHEWS.

THEY TOOK OVER THE SITE OF TWO BRISTOL TRAMWAYS SHEDS AT FILTON, IN WHAT IS NOW SOUTH GLOUCESTERSHIRE. A *ZODIAC* BIPLANE WAS SENT OVER FROM FRANCE — BUT IT *WOULDN'T FLY!*

PUSH IT TO THE BACK OF THE HANGAR AND FORGET IT!

NOT ONE TO BE PUT OFF, GEORGE IMMEDIATELY TURNED TO A DIFFERENT AIRCRAFT DESIGN AND ON 30 JULY 1910 HIS FIRST AEROPLANE TOOK TO THE AIR!

THE *BRISTOL BIPLANE*, BETTER KNOWN AS THE *BOXKITE*, FLEW SPECTACULAR DISPLAYS OVER BRISTOL'S DOWNS IN NOVEMBER 1910.

GEORGE HAD TO CREATE A *MARKET* FOR THIS NEW PRODUCT, SO HE SET UP *FLYING SCHOOLS*. BY 1914 AROUND 80% OF THE QUALIFIED PILOTS IN BRITAIN HAD BEEN TRAINED IN BRISTOL AEROPLANES.

AFTER JUST A YEAR THOSE TWO TRAMSHEDS HAD TURNED INTO THE BIGGEST AIRCRAFT FACTORY IN THE WORLD, WITH 80 WORKERS. ONE JOURNALIST AT THE TIME WROTE:

THE B. AND C.A.C. WORKS PROPER WOULD MAKE MOST OF OUR CONSTRUCTORS GREEN WITH ENVY, SO BEAUTIFULLY ARE THEY PLANNED AND BUILT.

BY 1912, *WAR* WAS ON THE HORIZON AND WITH HIS USUAL FORESIGHT GEORGE PREDICTED...

BELIEVE ME, DURING THE NEXT FIVE YEARS THE POWERS WILL CALL FOR THOUSANDS, IF NOT TENS OF THOUSANDS, OF AIRPLANES AND THE DEVELOPMENTS IN THEIR USE FOR BOTH MILITARY AND NAVAL PURPOSES WILL BE STARTLING.

THE BRITISH & COLONIAL FACTORIES BUILT THOUSANDS OF AIRCRAFT FOR THE WAR EFFORT, INCLUDING: OVER 1200 *B.E.2S*...

... 376 *BRISTOL SCOUTS*...

... 130 *BRISTOL M1 MONOPLANES*

... AND THE FAMOUS *BRISTOL FIGHTER*, ALSO KNOWN AS 'BRISFIT'. OVER *4,700* WERE BUILT BY THE COMPANY AND AT OTHER FACTORIES IN THE UK.

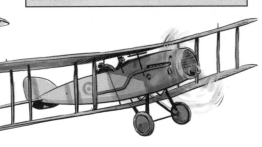

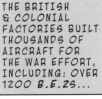

SIR GEORGE WHITE - THE BOXKITE BARONET

AS THE WAR CONTINUED, SIR GEORGE'S HEALTH WORSENED. CAROLINE DIED IN 1915 AND HE NEVER FULLY RECOVERED FROM THIS LOSS.

I AM SO TIRED.

THERE WERE BUSINESS TROUBLES TOO. HE HAD INVESTED £10,000 IN RESEARCH AND DEVELOPMENT FOR THE *PARAVANE*, AN INVENTION WHICH WOULD PROTECT SHIPS FROM UNDERWATER MINES.

NOW THE GOVERNMENT WANTED TO GIVE THE DESIGNS AWAY. SIR GEORGE WAS WORRIED THIS WOULD STOP THE LIFE-SAVING INVENTION GOING INTO PRODUCTION.

ON 22 NOVEMBER 1916 HE WAS TOLD THE GOVERNMENT WOULD LET HIM GO AHEAD WITH THE PARAVANE.

BUT SADLY, GEORGE WOULD NOT SEE IT GO INTO PRODUCTION. HE DIED AT HIS DESK THAT EVENING.

THE PARAVANE SAVED THE LIVES OF THOUSANDS OF SAILORS. MANY MORE PEOPLE WERE GRATEFUL TO GEORGE WHITE, AS THIS CARTOON BY BRISTOL ARTIST F.G. LEWIN SHOWS.

GEORGE WAS LAID TO REST WITH CAROLINE IN A VAULT AT ST MARY'S CHURCH, STOKE BISHOP. HE HAD WANTED A SIMPLE FUNERAL BUT THE CHURCHYARD WAS FULL OF MOURNERS.

A MEMORIAL AT BRISTOL CATHEDRAL ATTRACTED AN EVEN BIGGER GATHERING, INCLUDING POLITICIANS, V.I.P.S AND REPRESENTATIVES OF THE HOSPITALS HE HAD BUILT AND THE CHARITIES HE HAD HELPED. CROWDS STOOD OUTSIDE AND TRAMS DRAPED IN BLACK RIBBONS CAME TO A RESPECTFUL STOP. FOR A MOMENT IT SEEMED THAT THE WHOLE CITY HAD PAUSED TO REMEMBER SIR GEORGE.

GEORGE WHITE WAS ALIVE AT A TIME OF GREAT TECHNOLOGICAL CHANGE. HE SAW HOW NEW INVENTIONS COULD BE TURNED INTO BUSINESSES THAT MADE A BIG DIFFERENCE TO PEOPLE'S LIVES.

THE BRISTOL AVIATION INDUSTRY WHICH HE STARTED HAS GROWN INTO AN INTERNATIONAL SUCCESS STORY. SOME OF THE WORLD'S MOST FAMOUS AIRCRAFT STARTED LIFE ON THE SITE OF THE TWO TRAMSHEDS WHERE GEORGE BUILT HIS FIRST AEROPLANES.

THE CHARLES ROLLS STORY

2ND JUNE 1910. DOVER.

LOOK!

HERE COMES ROLLS!

HURRAH!

GOOD SHOW!

BRAVO!

CHARLES ROLLS WAS THE FIRST AEROPLANE PILOT TO MAKE A NON-STOP RETURN FLIGHT ACROSS THE ENGLISH CHANNEL. THIS WAS JUST ONE OF THE MANY ADVENTURES AND ACHIEVEMENTS OF HIS SHORT LIFE...

CHARLES STEWART ROLLS WAS BORN IN LONDON IN 1877. NEWS OF HIS BIRTH *MAY* HAVE BEEN DELIVERED BY A MESSENGER BOY CALLED *HENRY ROYCE*.

IT *COULD* BE TRUE, WE'LL NEVER KNOW...

HIS FATHER, LORD LLANGATTOCK, WAS MP FOR MONMOUTHSHIRE AND CHARLES GREW UP AT *THE HENDRE*, THE GRAND FAMILY HOME NEAR MONMOUTH. FROM AN EARLY AGE HE WAS FASCINATED BY MACHINES.

FATHER, WHEN SHALL *I* BE BIG ENOUGH TO RIDE YOUR HIGH-WHEELER?

LIKE HIS WEALTHY FATHER, CHARLES WENT TO ETON AND CAMBRIDGE. AT UNIVERSITY HE STUDIED ENGINEERING, RACED BICYCLES AND EVEN VISITED FRANCE TO BECOME THE FIRST *CAR-OWNING STUDENT!*

THE ENGINE IS *3.75 HORSEPOWER*, MONSIEUR. ONE OF THE *FINEST* IN THE WORLD.

I'LL TAKE IT!

ONE OF THE FIRST CAR-OWNERS IN BRITAIN, CHARLES *HATED* THE SPEED LIMIT OF 4 MILES PER HOUR.

SIR! YOU'RE SUPPOSED TO DRIVE *BEHIND* THE FLAG!

SORRY! HAVEN'T GOT ALL DAY!

HE JOINED THE SELF PROPELLED TRAFFIC ASSOCIATION, WHICH GOT THE LIMIT RAISED. TO *12MPH!*

IN 1902 CHARLES SET UP *CS ROLLS & CO.*, USING SOME OF HIS FATHER'S MONEY. FROM HIS LONDON SHOWROOM HE SOLD CARS TO THE FEW WHO WERE RICH ENOUGH TO AFFORD THEM. MOST OF THE CARS CAME FROM OVERSEAS.

I SIMPLY *CAN'T* FIND ANY BRITISH-MADE CAR I REALLY LIKE.

COME TO *MANCHESTER* WITH ME, CHARLES. I'LL CHANGE YOUR MIND!

HIS FRIEND EDMUNDS KNEW JUST THE PERSON TO HELP.

4TH MAY, 1904. MIDLAND HOTEL, MANCHESTER.

CHARLES, MAY I INTRODUCE *HENRY ROYCE* OF ROYCE & CO. HENRY, THIS IS THE HONOURABLE CHARLES ROLLS.

IT IS MY AMBITION TO HAVE A MOTOR CAR CONNECTED WITH MY NAME, SO THAT IN FUTURE IT MIGHT BE A *HOUSEHOLD WORD*.

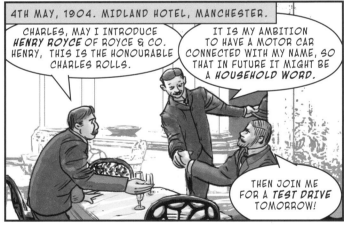

THEN JOIN ME FOR A *TEST DRIVE* TOMORROW!

MAGNIFICENT! I'LL HAVE NO TROUBLE SELLING THESE, ROYCE. SEND ME *EVERY CAR YOU CAN MAKE!*

HENRY ROYCE WAS A HARD-WORKING ENGINEER WHO HAD FACED SEVERE POVERTY. HE WAS NOTHING LIKE THE ARISTOCRATIC CHARLES ROLLS, BUT THE PAIR GOT ON WELL.

IN 1906, *ROLLS-ROYCE* WAS BORN.

HENRY WORKED ON THE CARS WHILE CHARLES ATTRACTED ATTENTION TO THE NEW COMPANY. TO SHOW JUST HOW GOOD THEIR CARS WERE, CHARLES DECIDED TO DRIVE THEM IN COMPETITIONS. *BUT IN THE FIRST RACE...*

CRACK!

IT'S THE GEARBOX, SIR.

SABOTAGE!

LUCKILY FOR THE COMPANY, ANOTHER ROLLS-ROYCE CAR PERFORMED WELL IN THE RACE.

A YEAR LATER CHARLES WON THE SAME RACE, AND *MANY OTHERS.*

THE CREDIT IS DUE TO MR ROYCE, THE DESIGNER.

AUTOMOBILE CLUB OF GREAT BRITAIN AND IRELAND
119 PICCADILLY, LONDON, W.
Certificate of Performance
Under the Open Competition Rules of the A.C.G.B.I.

THE INTERNATIONAL
TOURIST TROPHY RACE
Held in the Isle of Man.—September 27th, 1906.

This is to Certify that the 20 h.p. Rolls-R—
Car, entered by The Hon C.S. Rolls
and driven by him
successfully completed the Course of 161 miles 240 yards, and
placed First, twenty-nine Cars having started.

ROLLS ROYCE

THE BEST SIX-CYLINDER CAR IN THE WORLD?

HIS RACING FAME WAS GOOD FOR BUSINESS. BY 1910 A NEW FACTORY IN DERBY WAS MAKING *300* CARS A YEAR.

CHARLES WAS ALSO A SUCCESSFUL *BALLOONIST.*

RACE YOU BACK TO MONMOUTH!

ONE OF THE FIRST MEMBERS OF THE AERO CLUB OF GREAT BRITAIN, HE WON A GOLD MEDAL FOR SPENDING THE LONGEST TIME IN THE AIR. THERE WAS EVEN A TROPHY FOR THE BALLOONIST WHO COULD LAND NEAREST HIS HOME IN MONMOUTHSHIRE!

BUT CHARLES WAS ALWAYS LOOKING FOR MORE *EXCITING* WAYS TO TRAVEL.

I WANT MORE *CONTROL*, THE WIND'S TOO UNPREDICTABLE.

WOULDN'T MIND ONE OF THOSE *WRIGHT BROTHERS* FLYING MACHINES...

ORVILLE AND *WILBUR WRIGHT* WERE AMERICAN INVENTORS, WHO MADE THE FIRST POWERED, CONTROLLED FLIGHT IN THE HISTORY OF AVIATION. WILBUR WAS TRYING TO SELL THE RIGHTS TO THEIR AEROPLANE, *THE FLYER*, WHEN CHARLES MET HIM IN FRANCE.

I COULD SELL *A LOT* OF THESE FOR YOU IN BRITAIN. WHAT DO YOU SAY?

I'LL HAVE TO ASK *ORVILLE.*

WILBUR DID GIVE CHARLES A RIDE IN HIS *FLYER.*

IT WAS THE REALISATION OF SEVERAL DREAMS AND I COULD THINK OF NOTHING ELSE FOR A LONG WHILE.

CHARLES BECAME ONLY THE SECOND PERSON IN BRITAIN TO QUALIFY AS A PILOT. BUT HIS LOVE OF FLYING WOULD END TRAGICALLY...

THE CHARLES ROLLS STORY

IN 1910, ONLY A FEW WEEKS AFTER HIS TRIUMPHANT CHANNEL CROSSING, CHARLES WAS COMPETING IN AN AIRSHOW IN BOURNEMOUTH.

HE WAS PILOTING A WRIGHT BROTHERS *FLYER*, WHICH HE HAD ADAPTED HIMSELF.

DURING A STEEP DIVE, THE TAIL SUDDENLY *BROKE OFF*.

THERE WAS NOTHING CHARLES COULD DO. THE FLYER CRASHED TO THE GROUND, IN FRONT OF THE HORRIFIED SPECTATORS.

HE WAS ONLY *32* YEARS OLD, THE FIRST BRITISH PERSON TO BE KILLED IN AN AEROPLANE CRASH.

HIS BODY WAS RETURNED TO MONMOUTHSHIRE AND HE WAS BURIED AT LLANGATTOCK VIBON AVEL CHURCH.

TODAY, ROLLS-ROYCE PRODUCES SOME OF THE WORLD'S MOST POWERFUL AND SUCCESSFUL ENGINES AT ITS FACTORIES IN FILTON, DERBY AND OVERSEAS.

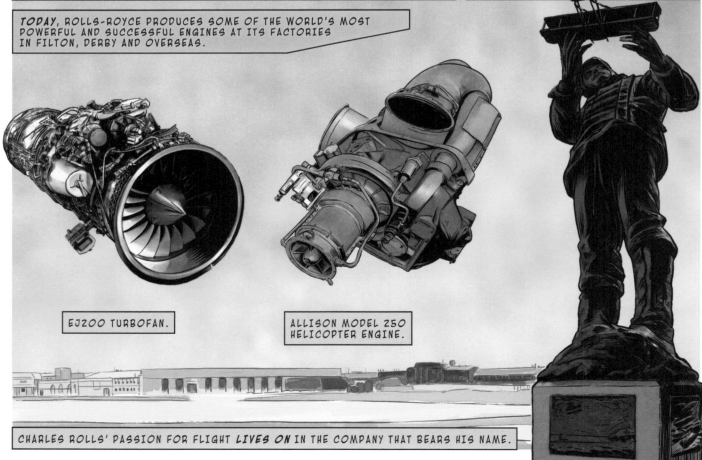

EJ200 TURBOFAN.

ALLISON MODEL 250 HELICOPTER ENGINE.

CHARLES ROLLS' PASSION FOR FLIGHT *LIVES ON* IN THE COMPANY THAT BEARS HIS NAME.

What else was going on in 1910, the year George White set up his company and Charles Rolls died in an aeroplane crash?

The Milan Aviation Meeting, Italy, 1910
(SCIENCE AND SOCIETY PICTURE LIBRARY/SCIENCE MUSEUM PICTORIAL).

The World in 1910

Well, in aviation lots of exciting things were happening. It was only seven years since the Wright brothers had made their first flight but designs for aeroplanes were getting better and better.

In 1910 the first seaplane was designed and flown in France by Henri Fabre. The first aeroplane with two engines instead of one was being tested and an aeroplane took off from the deck of a ship for the first time. In October Henri Coanda's Coanda-1910 was the first serious attempt to make a jet-propelled aeroplane. Coanda was ahead of his time but the aeroplane only flew a little way before it crashed to the ground. It was a clever idea and he almost got it to work.

More and more people were becoming pilots. In France Baroness de Laroche became the world's first qualified female pilot – this means she had passed the official tests and was given a licence. John Theodore Cuthbert Moore-Brabazon became the first person in Britain to qualify (remember that Charles Rolls was the second). Edith Maud Cook became the first British woman to fly solo, but sadly she died later that year. She was killed at a fairground when she tried to jump out of a balloon using a parachute.

Claude Grahame-White made the first night flight in Europe. This took place in April during a race from London to Manchester. He had only a few faint lights on the ground to guide him and this was long before the days of radar, so it was a very brave thing to do. He was flying a Farman biplane that was designed and built in France. A pilot called Louis Paulhan was also flying a biplane from the Farman company. Paulhan won the race and the £10,000 prize. In October Grahame-White took his biplane to America (by ship, of course, as aeroplanes couldn't fly that far then). He caused a sensation when he landed on a road near the White House where the President lived.

In July 1910 Léon Morane became the first person to fly at more than 100km an hour (that's about 62 miles per hour). In September Georges Legagneux flew higher than anyone before, reaching 3,100 metres. He broke the record again in 1914 when he got to 6,150 metres – and this was at a time before cockpits were enclosed, so it was bloomin' cold up there. In November 1910 the French pilot Maurice Tabuteau flew 586km non-stop, setting a new world record for distance flying.

The first cargo flight took place when Philip Parmalee used a Wright brothers' aeroplane to transport a stock of silk cloth for the owner of a department store in Ohio. The store owner sold tickets for people to see the aeroplane land and also sold strips of the silk as souvenirs.

Georges Chavez from Peru made the first flight over the Swiss Alps. Unfortunately he didn't get a chance to celebrate as he was fatally injured when his Blériot monoplane crashed on landing.

1910 was also the year of the first mid-air collision between two aeroplanes (no-one was killed, thank goodness).

What else was happening? In Britain the Edwardian era came to an end when King Edward VII died suddenly. He was succeeded by his son George V. Halley's Comet was seen for the first time since 1835. Suffragettes were fighting for votes for women, and the Girl Guide movement was started by Lady Baden-Powell.

Some of Britain's first cinemas were opening in towns and cities across the country. The films were silent in those days but the cinemas usually had live music playing to add to the excitement. It was also the year the British comedian Charlie Chaplin left London for America. Within ten years he was the most famous film star in the world.

The *Olympic* was launched in Belfast by the White Star Line. She was a big, luxurious ocean liner, and the world's heaviest man-made object. Her sister ship, *Titanic*, was launched – and sank – two years later.

The scientist Marie Curie published her work on radioactivity. The explorer Captain Scott began his expedition to the South Pole. There was a revolution in Mexico, Mount Etna erupted in Italy and the nurse Florence Nightingale died at the age of 90.

There was a census carried out in 1911 which gives us a picture of how people were living at that time. Britain had a population of about 37 million people – there are about 60 million living here now. Women could expect to live to the age of 54 and men to the age of 50. Now the average life expectancy is 81 for women and 76 for men. Things have improved because most of us have access to better food, medicine, sanitation and housing than they did then. Most of us also work in less dangerous and unhealthy jobs.

1910 fashion advert (© VICTORIA & ALBERT MUSEUM, LONDON).

The Nice Aviation Meeting, France, 1910 (SCIENCE AND SOCIETY PICTURE LIBRARY/SCIENCE MUSEUM PICTORIAL).

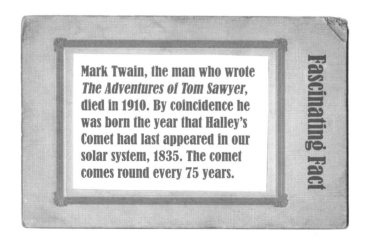

Mark Twain, the man who wrote *The Adventures of Tom Sawyer*, died in 1910. By coincidence he was born the year that Halley's Comet had last appeared in our solar system, 1835. The comet comes round every 75 years.

Fascinating Fact

Early Charlie Chaplin film poster (© VICTORIA & ALBERT MUSEUM, LONDON).

COME WITH US ON A JOURNEY THROUGH THE HISTORY OF *TRANSPORT*. IT'S A *MOVING* TALE!

IN THE BEGINNING WE HUMANS HAD TO CARRY THINGS OURSELVES...

THEN WE HAD THE CLEVER IDEA OF LETTING ANIMALS DO THE HARD WORK!

MOMENTS

BUT TRANSPORT DIDN'T REALLY GET ROLLING UNTIL THE INVENTION OF *THE WHEEL*. SUDDENLY IT WAS POSSIBLE TO MAKE ANIMALS CARRY EVEN HEAVIER GOODS AND MORE PEOPLE.

THANKS A LOT!

5,500 YEARS AGO

AS FAR AS WE KNOW, THE FIRST PEOPLE TO USE WHEELS WERE THE MESOPOTAMIANS (IN WHAT IS NOW IRAQ). BUT THESE WERE *POTTERS'* WHEELS - IT'S LIKELY THAT *VEHICLE* WHEELS DIDN'T APPEAR FOR ANOTHER THREE HUNDRED YEARS.

THERE MUST BE A BETTER WAY OF GETTING MY POTS TO MARKET!

5,200 YEARS AGO

THE IDEA FOR THE WHEELED CART PROBABLY CAME ABOUT BY REPLACING THE RUNNERS OF A SLEDGE WITH *ROLLERS*. ROLLERS WERE USUALLY TREE TRUNKS, USED TO MOVE REALLY BIG, HEAVY THINGS LIKE ROCKS.

4,000 YEARS AGO

500 YEARS AGO

IT'S HARD TO BELIEVE, BUT THE WHEEL DIDN'T REACH NORTH OR SOUTH AMERICA UNTIL EUROPEANS ARRIVED IN THE LATE 15TH CENTURY.

THE FIRST WHEELS WERE JUST PLANKS OF WOOD CUT TO MAKE A DISC SHAPE. THE INTRODUCTION OF *SPOKES* (IN MESOPOTAMIA AGAIN) MADE VEHICLES LIGHTER AND FASTER.

SLEDGES CONTINUED TO BE USED IN SOME PLACES, EVEN THOUGH WHEELS WERE MORE EFFICIENT. IN 17TH CENTURY BRISTOL, CARTS WERE BANNED BECAUSE THE HEAVIER CARGO THEY COULD CARRY WAS A DANGER TO THE CITY'S UNDERGROUND CELLARS.

ROAD

THE GREATER *SPEED* OF SPOKED WHEELS MADE WAR CHARIOTS POSSIBLE. THIS COMPLETELY CHANGED THE FACE OF WARFARE!

THE ROAD TRANSPORT REVOLUTION

CHARIOTS WERE GOOD FOR WARFARE BUT TOO SMALL AND BUMPY FOR ANY OTHER PURPOSE. *CARTS* WERE LARGER, BUT COULD NOT BE STEERED EASILY BECAUSE THEIR WHEELS WERE FIXED. EVENTUALLY, *CARRIAGES* APPEARED, WITH *SPRUNG SUSPENSIONS* FOR COMFORT AND *PIVOTAL AXLES* FOR STEERING.

... NONE OF THEM COULD MOVE FASTER THAN THE ANIMAL PULLING IT.

GREATER DISTANCES COULD BE COVERED BY THE *STAGE COACH*, A TRANSPORT SYSTEM WHERE FRESH HORSES REPLACED TIRED ONES AT SET POINTS ON A LONG ROUTE.

A HORSE IS A SORT OF *LIVING ENGINE*. RUNNING ON FUEL OF FOOD AND WATER, IT PROVIDES THE *POWER* TO MOVE A VEHICLE. IN THE 19TH CENTURY NEW MACHINES AND NEW FUELS APPEARED WHICH FINALLY MADE THE 'HORSE-LESS CARRIAGE' POSSIBLE.

LATER, BIG VEHICLES LIKE THE OMNIBUS AND THE TRAM MEANT HORSES COULD CARRY MORE PEOPLE AT ONCE. BUT ALL THESE FORMS OF TRANSPORT SHARED ONE PROBLEM...

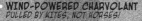

18	20	18	40	18	60	18	80	19	00

INVENTIONS

- MACADAM 3-LAYER ROAD
  SMOOTHER, LONGER-LASTING SURFACE
- VULCANIZATION • PNEUMATIC TYRE
  STRENGTHENED RUBBER FILLED WITH AIR, MADE TRAVEL MORE COMFORTABLE
- INTERNAL COMBUSTION ENGINE
  EXPLOSION MOVES PISTON WHICH CAN BE MADE TO TURN A WHEEL
- PETROL-DRIVEN ENGINE • DIESEL ENGINE
  LIGHTER AND MORE EFFICIENT THAN EARLIER ENGINES
- FORD'S MODEL T PRODUCTION LINE •
  MASS-PRODUCTION MADE CARS AFFORDABLE

VEHICLES

- ELECTRIC TRAM
  STILL USED TODAY IN SOME CITIES
- WIND-POWERED CHARVOLANT
  PULLED BY KITES, NOT HORSES!
- DRAISINE • PEDAL BICYCLE
  PEDAL-LESS BICYCLE
- PENNY FARTHING • SAFETY BICYCLE
  PEDALS LINKED TO WHEEL BY CHAIN
- STEAM-POWERED MOTORCYCLE
  SIZE AND WEIGHT OF STEAM ENGINE MADE FIRST MOTORBIKES UNSTABLE
- TRAM ENGINE
  STEAM LOCOMOTIVE FOR ROADS
- BENZ MOTORWAGON
  THREE-WHEELED, PETROL-DRIVEN MOTOR CAR
- DAIMLER/MAYBECH FOUR-WHEELED • PETROL-DRIVEN CAR

18	20	18	40	18	60	18	80	19	00

IN TRANSPORT HISTORY

MEANWHILE *AT SEA*, TRANSPORT HAD COME A LONG WAY SINCE THE FIRST *CANOES* CARVED OUT OF LOGS.

AT LEAST **6,000 YEARS AGO** SINGLE-MASTED *SAILING SHIPS* HAD HARNESSED *WIND POWER*. EGYPT AND MESOPOTAMIA NEEDED SHIPS SO THEY COULD *TRADE* WITH COUNTRIES ACROSS THE SEA (THEIR ENEMIES HAD BETTER WEAPONS, MADE OF *BRONZE* AND TO MAKE BRONZE YOU NEED TIN AND COPPER, WHICH THEY DIDN'T HAVE.)

HOW DID THESE TRADING SHIPS FIND THE COPPER-SELLERS OF CYPRUS AND THE TIN MERCHANTS OF SPAIN? THEY MUST HAVE HAD *MAPS* OF SOME KIND. THE EARLIEST KNOWN MAP OF THE WORLD COMES FROM MESOPOTAMIA **3,000 YEARS AGO.**

MAPS AND CHARTS ARE ONLY USEFUL IF YOU CAN MATCH THEM TO YOUR ACTUAL POSITION. THAT'S WHERE *NAVIGATION* COMES IN. THE EARLIEST NAVIGATORS USED LANDMARKS AND THE STARS TO STAY ON COURSE.

THE *MAGNETIC COMPASS* (**900 YEARS AGO**) MADE IT EASIER FOR SAILORS TO KNOW WHICH *DIRECTION* THEY WERE GOING. INSTRUMENTS LIKE THE ASTROLABE AND *SEXTANT* (**1667**) TOLD NAVIGATORS THEIR *LATITUDE* (DISTANCE NORTH OR SOUTH OF THE EQUATOR)...

...BUT FINDING THE *LONGITUDE* (EAST-WEST POSITION) WAS FAR HARDER, UNTIL THE SUCCESSFUL TRIALS OF THE *MARINE CHRONOMETER* IN **1761**

MUCH LATER, IN **1960**, THE FIRST *SATELLITE NAVIGATION SYSTEM* WAS TESTED, EVENTUALLY LEADING TO THE *GLOBAL POSITIONING SYSTEM*. GPS USES PRECISE TIMINGS FROM A NETWORK OF SATELLITES TO CALCULATE RELIABLE POSITIONS.

SEA

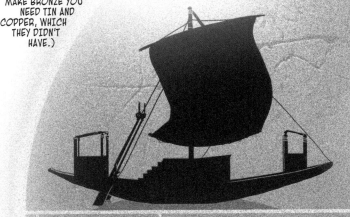

4,500 YEARS AGO

3,200 YEARS AGO

1,800 YEARS AGO

7TH CENTURY

15TH CENTURY

1620

19TH CENTURY

1801

1802

1838

1845

1954

1959

4,500 YEARS AGO EGYPTIAN SEA VESSEL *FLEXIBLE HULL* MADE FROM SHORT TIMBERS.

3,200 YEARS AGO MEDITERRANEAN TRADING SHIP *RIGID HULL* STRENGTHENED BY *RIBS* (HEAVY BEAMS ACROSS HULL WIDTH).

1,800 YEARS AGO ROMAN BARGE TRIANGULAR SAILS SET *FORE AND AFT* (ALONG A SHIP'S LENGTH) MADE IT POSSIBLE TO HEAD ALMOST 45° TO AN ONCOMING WIND. BEFORE, SHIPS HAD NEEDED THE WIND BEHIND THEM TO MOVE FORWARD.

7TH CENTURY CHINESE JUNK SEVERAL MASTS FOR LARGER SAIL AREA AND A CENTRAL RUDDER.

15TH CENTURY EUROPEAN THREE-MASTED SHIP BIGGER AND FASTER THANKS TO THE SIZE AND NUMBER OF THEIR SAILS.

1620 THE FIRST SUBMARINE DRIVEN BY UNDERWATER OARS.

19TH CENTURY CLIPPER *GREATER SAIL AREA AND STREAM-LINED HULL* DESIGN MADE LONG VOYAGES MUCH FASTER.

1801 FULTON'S SUBMARINE CONTROLLED DEPTH WITH *BALLAST TANKS.*

1802 CHARLOTTE DUNDAS THE FIRST *PADDLE-STEAMER* TO ACHIEVE COMMERCIAL SUCCESS.

1838 SS GREAT WESTERN DESIGNED TO BE BIG ENOUGH TO CARRY THE COAL NEEDED FOR LONG TRIPS.

1845 SS GREAT BRITAIN BIG, IRON-HULLED AND DRIVEN BY A SCREW PROPELLER - SHE WAS THE FIRST MODERN SHIP.

1954 NUCLEAR-POWERED SUBMARINE NUCLEAR FUEL GIVES VESSELS ALMOST UNLIMITED RANGE.

1959 SR.N1 THE FIRST FULL-SIZE HOVERCRAFT, INVENTED BY CHRISTOPHER COCKERELL. A RUBBER SKIRT WAS LATER ADDED, WHICH ENABLED THE HOVERCRAFT TO CROSS ROUGH SEAS.

STEAM POWER, WHICH TRANSFORMED SHIPS IN THE 19TH CENTURY, CAUSED ANOTHER TRANSPORT REVOLUTION ON DRY LAND...

IN **1712** THOMAS NEWCOMEN MADE A MACHINE WHICH COULD MOVE A *PISTON* UP AND DOWN USING *STEAM POWER.* HE CALLED IT *THE ATMOSPHERIC STEAM-ENGINE.*

IN **1769** JAMES WATT ADAPTED THE STEAM-ENGINE TO TURN WHEELS, BUT IT WASN'T UNTIL **1804** THAT STEAM WAS APPLIED TO *RAIL TRANSPORT.*

RICHARD TREVITHICK'S *STEAM LOCOMOTIVE* WAS DESIGNED FOR USE IN THE COAL INDUSTRY. IN LONDON IN **1808** TREVITHICK DEMONSTRATED A LOCOMOTIVE CALLED *CATCH ME WHO CAN*, BUT HE COULDN'T FIND INVESTORS WILLING TO HELP HIM DEVELOP THE INVENTION.

IN **1814** GEORGE STEPHENSON BUILT *THE BLUCHER,* HIS FIRST STEAM LOCOMOTIVE. HE WAS ENGINEER FOR *THE STOCKTON & DARLINGTON RAILWAY,* AND DESIGNED THE LINE TO RUN ON STEAM. WHEN IT WAS COMPLETED IN **1825** IT BECAME *THE FIRST PUBLIC STEAM RAILWAY* IN THE WORLD. IN **1829,** WITH HIS SON ROBERT, STEPHENSON BUILT *THE ROCKET,* THE MOST FAMOUS EARLY LOCOMOTIVE.

PEOPLE OR ANIMALS HAD BEEN PULLING WHEELED VEHICLES ALONG RAILS FOR CENTURIES BEFORE TREVITHICK'S STEAM LOCOMOTIVE.

2,600 YEARS AGO THE *DIOLKOS,* A PAVED TRACK WITH PARALLEL GROOVES, ENABLED SHIPS TO BE HAULED ACROSS THE ISTHMUS OF CORINTH FROM THE IONIAN SEA TO THE AEGEAN SEA.

RAIL

IN *THE 1830S* THE SUCCESS OF STEAM LOCOMOTIVE DESIGN CAUSED A VAST NETWORK OF RAILWAY LINES TO APPEAR, INCLUDING BRUNEL'S *GREAT WESTERN RAILWAY (GWR).*

1840 GWR STANDARDISED *RAILWAY TIME* TO STOP TIMETABLE CONFUSION CAUSED BY BRISTOL CLOCKS RUNNING TEN MINUTES BEHIND LONDON.

BY THE *14TH CENTURY* HORSE-DRAWN CARTS ON TRACKS WERE A POPULAR WAY OF MOVING HEAVY LOADS LIKE COAL. EVEN BEFORE STEAM ENGINES, IT WAS EASIER TO MOVE WAGONS ALONG TWO SMOOTH RAILS THAN TO STRUGGLE ALONG BUMPY ROADS.

fig. 1

fig. 2

1863 FIRST UNDERGROUND RAIL SERVICE, THE METROPOLITAN RAILWAY, LONDON.

1869 EAST AND WEST COASTS OF THE USA CONNECTED BY RAIL.

IN 1825 THE HORSE-DRAWN *CHESHUNT RAILWAY* OPENED, BECOMING THE WORLD'S FIRST *PASSENGER MONORAIL.* A SINGLE RAIL WAS CHEAPER THAN TWO, BUT LESS STABLE. A PAIR OF PARALLEL TRACKS HAS ALWAYS BEEN THE MOST WIDESPREAD TYPE OF RAILWAY, ALTHOUGH THE WIDTH OR *GAUGE* VARIES GREATLY.

1879 FIRST ELECTRIC RAILWAY, BERLIN.

1912 FIRST DIESEL-POWERED LOCOMOTIVE, WINTERTHUR-ROMANSHORN, SWITZERLAND.

1938 WORLD SPEED RECORD (STEAM LOCOMOTIVE) *203 KM/H* BY *MALLARD.*

1987 WORLD SPEED RECORD (DIESEL LOCOMOTIVE) *238 KM/H* BY *INTER-CITY 125.*

1990 WORLD SPEED RECORD (ELECTRIC) *515 KM/H* BY *TGV.*

1994 OPENING OF EUROSTAR PASSENGER SERVICE, LINKING THE UNITED KINGDOM AND FRANCE THROUGH THE *CHANNEL TUNNEL.*

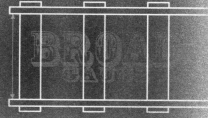

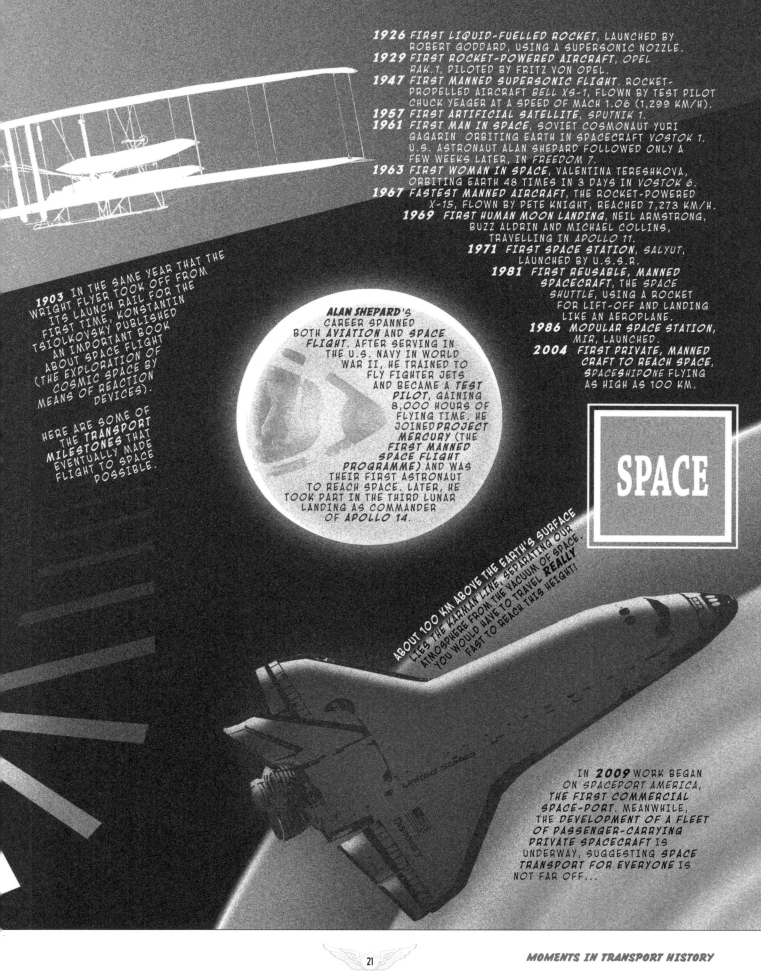

1926 FIRST LIQUID-FUELLED ROCKET, LAUNCHED BY ROBERT GODDARD, USING A SUPERSONIC NOZZLE.

1929 FIRST ROCKET-POWERED AIRCRAFT, OPEL RAK.1, PILOTED BY FRITZ VON OPEL.

1947 FIRST MANNED SUPERSONIC FLIGHT. ROCKET-PROPELLED AIRCRAFT BELL XS-1, FLOWN BY TEST PILOT CHUCK YEAGER AT A SPEED OF MACH 1.06 (1,299 KM/H).

1957 FIRST ARTIFICIAL SATELLITE, SPUTNIK 1.

1961 FIRST MAN IN SPACE, SOVIET COSMONAUT YURI GAGARIN, ORBITING EARTH IN SPACECRAFT VOSTOK 1. U.S. ASTRONAUT ALAN SHEPARD FOLLOWED ONLY A FEW WEEKS LATER, IN FREEDOM 7.

1963 FIRST WOMAN IN SPACE, VALENTINA TERESHKOVA, ORBITING EARTH 48 TIMES IN 3 DAYS IN VOSTOK 6.

1967 FASTEST MANNED AIRCRAFT, THE ROCKET-POWERED X-15, FLOWN BY PETE KNIGHT, REACHED 7,273 KM/H.

1969 FIRST HUMAN MOON LANDING, NEIL ARMSTRONG, BUZZ ALDRIN AND MICHAEL COLLINS, TRAVELLING IN APOLLO 11.

1971 FIRST SPACE STATION, SALYUT, LAUNCHED BY U.S.S.R.

1981 FIRST REUSABLE, MANNED SPACECRAFT, THE SPACE SHUTTLE, USING A ROCKET FOR LIFT-OFF AND LANDING LIKE AN AEROPLANE.

1986 MODULAR SPACE STATION, MIR, LAUNCHED.

2004 FIRST PRIVATE, MANNED CRAFT TO REACH SPACE, SPACESHIPONE FLYING AS HIGH AS 100 KM.

1903 IN THE SAME YEAR THAT THE WRIGHT FLYER TOOK OFF FROM ITS LAUNCH RAIL FOR THE FIRST TIME, KONSTANTIN TSIOLKOVSKY PUBLISHED AN IMPORTANT BOOK ABOUT SPACE FLIGHT (THE EXPLORATION OF COSMIC SPACE BY MEANS OF REACTION DEVICES).

HERE ARE SOME OF THE **TRANSPORT MILESTONES** THAT EVENTUALLY MADE FLIGHT TO SPACE POSSIBLE.

ALAN SHEPARD'S CAREER SPANNED BOTH **AVIATION** AND **SPACE FLIGHT**. AFTER SERVING IN THE U.S. NAVY IN WORLD WAR II, HE TRAINED TO FLY FIGHTER JETS AND BECAME A **TEST PILOT**, GAINING 8,000 HOURS OF FLYING TIME. HE JOINED **PROJECT MERCURY** (THE **FIRST MANNED SPACE FLIGHT PROGRAMME**) AND WAS THEIR FIRST ASTRONAUT TO REACH SPACE. LATER, HE TOOK PART IN THE THIRD LUNAR LANDING AS COMMANDER OF APOLLO 14.

SPACE

ABOUT 100 KM ABOVE THE EARTH'S SURFACE LIES THE KARMAN LINE, SEPARATING OUR ATMOSPHERE FROM THE VACUUM OF SPACE. YOU WOULD HAVE TO TRAVEL **REALLY** FAST TO REACH THIS HEIGHT!

IN **2009** WORK BEGAN ON SPACEPORT AMERICA, **THE FIRST COMMERCIAL SPACE-PORT**. MEANWHILE, THE DEVELOPMENT OF A FLEET OF PASSENGER-CARRYING PRIVATE SPACECRAFT IS UNDERWAY, SUGGESTING **SPACE TRANSPORT FOR EVERYONE** IS NOT FAR OFF...

MOMENTS IN TRANSPORT HISTORY

THE
LOCOMOTIVE ENGINE

This cutaway picture comes from the 19th century. It was used in classrooms to explain how energy from steam could power a railway locomotive. A steam train was the fastest way to travel on land in those days – much faster than the coach and horses that had been used before. For a lot of people, it was as amazing and exciting to travel by train as it would be for people today to travel in a space ship (PRIVATE COLLECTION).

Heat from the fire box produces hot gases which are carried along pipes through the boiler to heat the water to make the steam.

The steam whistle is used as a signal.

The safety valve lets steam out if the pressure is too high in the boiler.

MAN HOLE

STEAM WHISTLE

SAFETY 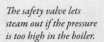 VALVE

FEED PIPE

DRIVING

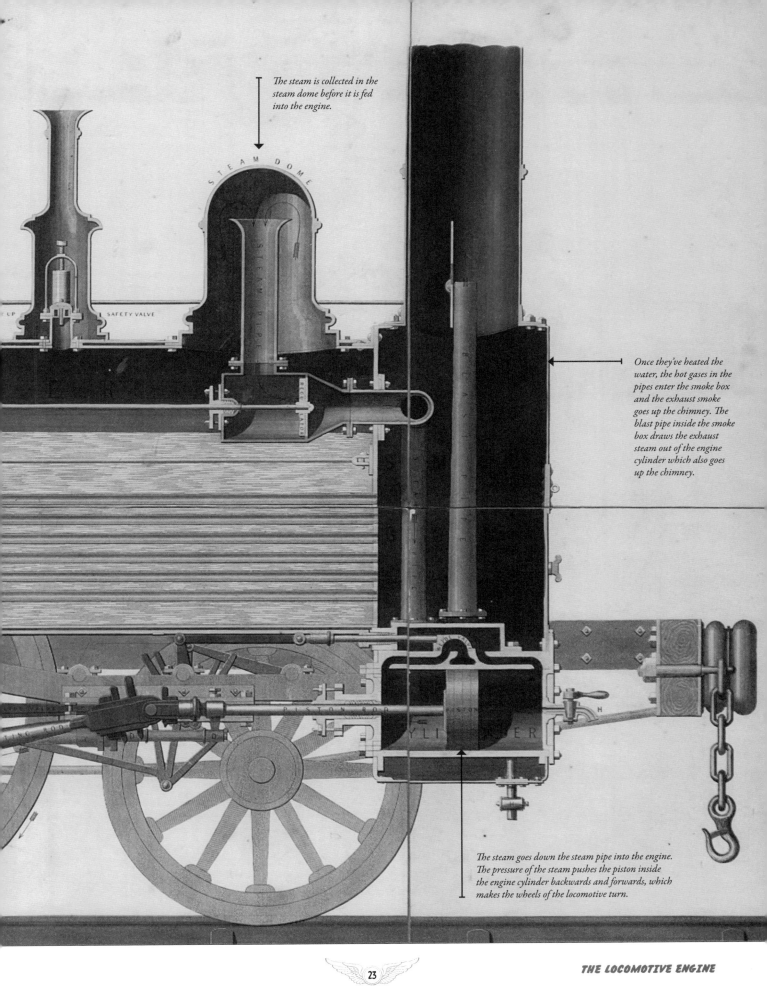

The steam is collected in the steam dome before it is fed into the engine.

Once they've heated the water, the hot gases in the pipes enter the smoke box and the exhaust smoke goes up the chimney. The blast pipe inside the smoke box draws the exhaust steam out of the engine cylinder which also goes up the chimney.

The steam goes down the steam pipe into the engine. The pressure of the steam pushes the piston inside the engine cylinder backwards and forwards, which makes the wheels of the locomotive turn.

THE LOCOMOTIVE ENGINE

DREAMS OF FLIGHT

FOR THOUSANDS OF YEARS, PEOPLE HAD LOOKED UP AT THE SKY, SEEN THE BIRDS OVERHEAD AND WISHED THAT THEY COULD FLY TOO.

Icarus pictured in the *Boy's Own Annual 1910* (BRISTOL LIBRARIES).

One of the world's oldest stories is the legend of Icarus. His father was a Greek inventor and architect called Daedalus. The King of Crete asked Daedalus to build a labyrinth where the Minotaur – a monster who was half-man, half-bull – was to be kept hidden (the Minotaur was the Queen's son but that's a story we'll save for another day). The King didn't want Daedalus to leave Crete – he was worried he would tell people the secret of the labyrinth – so Daedalus built wings for himself and Icarus so they could escape the island. The wings were made from wax and feathers. Daedalus warned his son not to fly too close to the sun, but Icarus was so excited he ignored the warning. He flew high up into the sky and the wax on his wings was melted by the heat of the sun. He lost his feathers, plunged into the sea and was drowned.

Perhaps this legend was told to warn people to stop having foolish dreams about flying, but it didn't do any good because those dreams kept coming.

Kites were invented hundreds of years ago, probably by the Chinese, and there were early experiments in building kites big enough to carry people. Some of the things learnt about flight from kites would be useful when it came to designing aeroplanes, but that happened much later.

Hundreds of years were also spent making artificial wings. People would fit these on their arms before jumping off of towers and other high places. They thought by flapping their arms up and down like a bird they would be able to fly. They were wrong. Humans don't have enough strength in their arms to keep themselves up in the air by their own power. Also, a bird is able to fly not only because of the way it moves its wings (and, incidentally, that's not just going up and down like the flappers thought) but also because of the way it uses the air to give itself 'lift' (you'll find out about lift later on in this book). So, a lot of brave but foolish people jumped to their deaths... or at least to some nasty bumps and bruises.

The artist and inventor Leonardo da Vinci drew designs for flying machines in the fifteenth century. He was still caught up by the flapping wings idea – he designed flapping-winged machines called ornithopters – but some of his designs might have worked if he had also been able to invent the materials and equipment to make them with. His drawings included the first pictures of parachutes and helicopters, and he was one of the first people to think about the *science* of flight.

Hot air balloons worked much better than flapping wings. Better still were balloons filled with gas or hydrogen. The first successful experiments with balloons took place in the eighteenth century. This was also the time when the word 'aeronaut' started to be used to describe people who flew – it comes from the Greek words for 'air' and 'sailor'.

The greatest of the early balloonists were the Montgolfier brothers from France. They started their experiments by holding paper bags over fires and watching the bags float away as they filled with warm air. The first person to fly a balloon in Britain was an Italian called Vincenzo Lunardi.

The ENGLISH BALLOON and Appendages
in which Mr. LUNARDI ascended into
the Atmosphere, from the Artillery Ground,
Sepr. 15 1784.

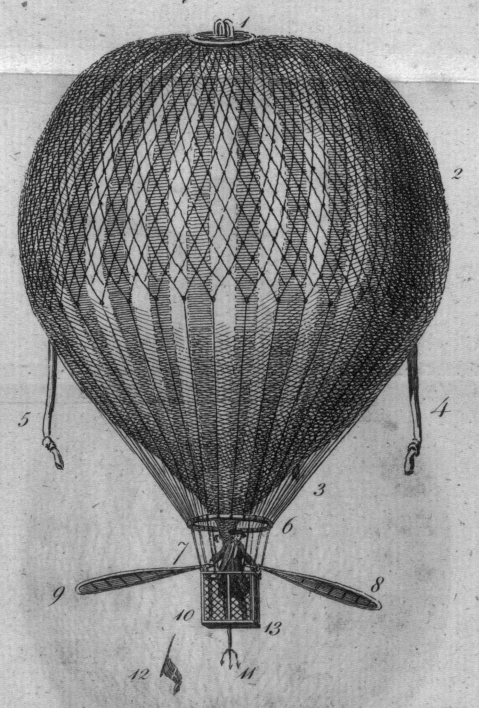

'Lunardi's balloon (UNIVERSITY OF BRISTOL LIBRARY, SPECIAL COLLECTIONS).

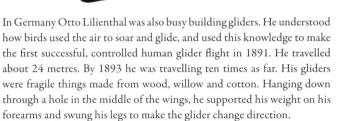

He was also known as the Daredevil Aeronaut. Unlike the Montgolfiers, he didn't really design balloons and he wasn't particularly scientific but he did become very famous for a while. His first flight took place on 15 September 1784 and was watched by a crowd of between 30,000 and 300,000 people (no one actually counted them all but there were an awful lot). The balloon was about ten metres in diameter. Lunardi had added rowing oars and flappable wings to the balloon's basket, which he thought would help him fly further (as we said, he wasn't very scientific). He floated over London, made a brief stop to drop off his cat that had been in the basket with him (!) and finally landed 40 kilometres from where he started. He made many more ascents around the country and was a national hero until the terrible day of 27 August 1786 when a young man got caught up in the ropes of his balloon, was carried into the air and fell to his death.

The problem with most kites and balloons is that the aeronaut can only really go where the air carries him or her. They fly because they are lighter than air. They don't have thrust – that's something you'll read more about later – and they can't be steered very easily (if at all).

In the nineteenth century, as people began to learn more about mechanics and engines, there were some experiments in powered *heavier-than-air* flight. In Britain engineers like George Cayley, William Henson and John Stringfellow tried to build special aero-engines to use in flying machines. They weren't very practical as at that time the pilots would have had to carry a large supply of water and coal, and a boiler to produce the steam that made the engines work. However, some of the things these men learnt from their experiments were very useful. Cayley, for example, built model gliders and from these he worked out the ideal shape for an aeroplane's wings. He also understood how rudders could be used to control direction and how an internal combustion engine (not yet invented) was needed to provide thrust. Henson and Stringfellow designed and built models that had propellers, rudders, elevators and wire-braced structures – you'll come across all of these again later in this book. In 1848 one of Stringfellow's steam-powered models became the first aeroplane in the world to fly (it was too small for anyone to sit in it).

In Germany Otto Lilienthal was also busy building gliders. He understood how birds used the air to soar and glide, and used this knowledge to make the first successful, controlled human glider flight in 1891. He travelled about 24 metres. By 1893 he was travelling ten times as far. His gliders were fragile things made from wood, willow and cotton. Hanging down through a hole in the middle of the wings, he supported his weight on his forearms and swung his legs to make the glider change direction.

Lilienthal influenced the Wright brothers – who have been mentioned a few times already – and he would have achieved much more if he hadn't been fatally injured in 1896. His glider crashed as he was trying to make a turn in a gust of wind. His motto was 'Sacrifices must be made'. He had certainly made the ultimate sacrifice for the sake of furthering science.

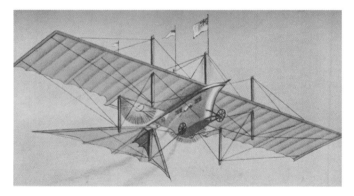

We're almost at 'proper' aeroplanes – not just models – but before we get there, let's go back a bit in history and talk about airships. We've said that the problem with balloons is that they usually just float wherever the air takes them. Airships were a big improvement on this. The first powered, lighter-than-air flight was made in an airship in 1852 by a Frenchman called Henri Giffard. By the end of the nineteenth century more and more airships were taking to the skies. They were long, cigar-shaped balloons that had engines and propellers to give them thrust, and rudders to steer with.

Until the 1930s airships were one of the most glamorous ways to travel. However, because they were filled with hydrogen gas they were highly flammable. This meant that when things went wrong they went *disastrously* wrong. On 6 May 1937 the Zeppelin company's *Hindenburg* airship burst into flames on arrival in New Jersey, USA. Film of the tragedy was shown all around the world and suddenly flying in an airship no longer seemed quite so much fun.

WHO WAS *PATRICK ALEXANDER*?

HAVE YOU HEARD OF PATRICK ALEXANDER? HE MIGHT BE BETTER KNOWN IF HE HAD STARTED A FAMOUS AEROPLANE COMPANY, LIKE GEORGE WHITE, OR IF HE'D BEEN KILLED IN THE AIR LIKE SO MANY PIONEERS. INSTEAD, HE LIVED A LONG LIFE, QUIETLY CONTRIBUTING TO AVIATION THROUGH HIS OWN EXPERIMENTS AND BY GENEROUSLY HELPING OTHERS.

PATRICK WAS BORN IN 1867, JUST A YEAR AFTER HIS FATHER HELPED TO FOUND THE *ROYAL AERONAUTICAL SOCIETY*. ANDREW ALEXANDER WAS A SUCCESSFUL ENGINEER WITH A KEEN INTEREST IN FLYING. HE HAD A MASSIVE INFLUENCE ON HIS SON.

HE SHOWED PATRICK AN ENORMOUS HYDROGEN BALLOON AT THE PARIS EXHIBITION OF 1878. HE CONVINCED HIS SON THAT POWERED FLIGHT WOULD OVERTAKE BALLOONING. AND HE WAS *WEALTHY*. WHEN HE DIED HE LEFT PATRICK THE EQUIVALENT OF MILLIONS OF POUNDS.

PATRICK COULD HARDLY WALK, AFTER BADLY BREAKING HIS LEG AT THE AGE OF 18, SO HE MIGHT HAVE CONSIDERED A QUIET, COMFORTABLE LIFE LIVING OFF HIS INHERITANCE. BUT HE CHOSE TO SPEND HIS ENTIRE FORTUNE ON *AVIATION*. HE PAID FOR HIS OWN EXPERIMENTS, FUNDED OTHER PEOPLE'S RESEARCH, BOUGHT HUGE BALLOONS AND TRAVELLED THE WORLD MEETING TOP AVIATORS (HE CROSSED THE ATLANTIC MORE THAN 50 TIMES!)

HE BUILT WORKSHOPS IN BATHEASTON TO TRY AND SOLVE THE PROBLEM OF BALLOON PROPULSION - HOW COULD YOU MAKE A HOT AIR BALLOON GO WHERE YOU WANTED? THIS WORK LED HIM TO GERMANY, WHERE HE WITNESSED THE MAIDEN FLIGHT OF GRAF ZEPPELIN'S AIRSHIP.

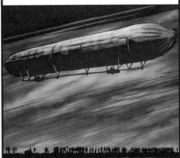

HE *NEARLY* ATTENDED AN EVEN BIGGER MOMENT IN AVIATION HISTORY - ORVILLE AND WILBUR WRIGHT'S FIRST FLIGHT AT KITTY HAWK - BUT THEIR TELEGRAM INVITATION NEVER REACHED HIM! TO MAKE MATTERS WORSE, PATRICK VISITED THE WRIGHT BROTHERS SO OFTEN THEY BEGAN TO SUSPECT HE WAS STEALING THEIR IDEAS!

DESPITE THIS MISUNDERSTANDING, PATRICK WAS LIKED AND RESPECTED BY THE WRIGHTS AND MANY OTHER PIONEERS. HE HELPED TO FOUND *THE AERO CLUB OF GREAT BRITAIN* AND BROUGHT THE WORLD'S BEST FLYERS TOGETHER. IN THIS WAY HE CONTRIBUTED TO THE EXCHANGE OF IDEAS WHICH HELPED IMPROVE THE SCIENCE OF FLIGHT.

PATRICK CARRIED ON SPENDING VAST AMOUNTS OF MONEY ON AVIATION RESEARCH, OFFERING THE ALEXANDER AWARD FOR THE DEVELOPMENT OF A LIGHTWEIGHT AERO ENGINE. £1000 WAS AN ENORMOUS AMOUNT OF MONEY IN 1910!

£1,000 PRIZE FOR MOTO

At the September 30th meeting of the Aerial League, Mr. PATRICK ALEXANDER offered a generous prize of £1,000 for the first Britis built engine to meet certain criter The competition, jointly adminis tered by the Royal A.C., the Aero nautical Society of Great Britain, Aero Club of the U.K., and the Aerial League, will judge:

AFTER THE FIRST WORLD WAR, PATRICK'S MONEY FINALLY RAN OUT AND HE TURNED TO TEACHING. BY PASSING ON HIS AERONAUTICAL KNOWLEDGE TO THE STUDENTS OF THE IMPERIAL SERVICE COLLEGE HE WAS ABLE TO MAKE ONE FINAL IMPORTANT CONTRIBUTION TO AVIATION. HE DIED IN 1943, HAVING LIVED UP TO THE MOTTO ON HIS GRAVE, *"SOMETHING ATTEMPTED, SOMETHING DONE."*

MAKE A TISSUE PAPER BALLOON

A hot air balloon rises because its envelope is filled with air that is warmer than the air around it. Warm air has more energy and is less dense (lighter) than cooler air so it pushes against the sides of the envelope – inflating it – and the balloon floats up.

Gluing the tissue paper (above) and taking flight (right) (MARTIN CHAINEY/AIRBUS).

MATERIALS: four sheets of standard artist's tissue paper (35cm x 70cm); one sheet of tissue paper cut to make a square with four sides of 35cm each; glue stick; paper clips.

EQUIPMENT: ruler; pencil; scissors; hair dryer; paint stripper gun.

1. Fold one of the rectangular sheets of tissue in half, one short edge touching the other one.

2. Open it up then fold it with the long edges touching.

3. Keep it folded and place your ruler along one of the short edges.

4. Make a mark on the edge of the sheet 7.5cm from the fold.

5. Now use your ruler to draw a diagonal line from that mark to the end of the fold you made in Step 1.

6. Cut along this line and open the sheet up to get a shape like this.

7. Repeat these six steps for the other three sheets.

8. Glue the 35cm side of one of the four long sheets to one of the sides of the square.

9. Do this for the other three sheets, so each side of the square has a longer piece of tissue attached (see photo).

10. Now glue the longer sides to each other to form your balloon envelope with the square tissue at one end, and a smaller square-shaped gap at the bottom.

11. Pull out the sides as much as you can without tearing the tissue or breaking the glue seal. The only gap should be at the bottom.

12. If you are indoors, hold the balloon above the nozzle of a hairdryer; if you are outdoors, hold the balloon above the nozzle of a paint stipper gun. When you switch on the heat your balloon should take flight (see photo).

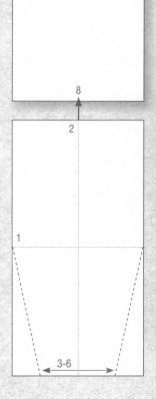

TIP

IF THE BALLOON IS UNSTABLE TRY ADDING A COUPLE OF PAPER CLIPS AROUND THE OPENING TO MAKE IT BALANCE.

HOW AEROPLANES FLY

➤ **THERE ARE FOUR FORCES THAT ACT ON AN AEROPLANE IN FLIGHT.**

LIFT – the upward aerodynamic force that comes from air moving over and under the aeroplane's wings.
WEIGHT – the downward force that comes from gravity.
THRUST – the forward force that comes from the aeroplane's engine exhaust or the propeller.
DRAG – the backward aerodynamic force that comes from the resistance caused by the aeroplane moving against the air.

We'll find out more about lifting and thrust later on. This picture shows forces acting on the Airbus A350 (AIRBUS).

Aeroplane pilots don't just want their aeroplane to stay up in the air. They need to be able to control the aeroplane's movement. The Wright brothers' flight in 1903 was so important because it was *controlled*. Controlled movement is safe and predictable. That's just what you want, when you are flying an aeroplane!

➤ **THERE ARE THREE SPECIAL WORDS TO DESCRIBE AN AEROPLANE'S MOVEMENT.**

ROLL – movement around the axis which runs from the aeroplane's nose to its tail.
YAW – movement around the axis which runs from the top of the aeroplane to the bottom.
PITCH – movement around the axis which runs from one wing tip to the other.

This picture shows where the three axes cross on the Bristol Blenheim (AIRBUS).

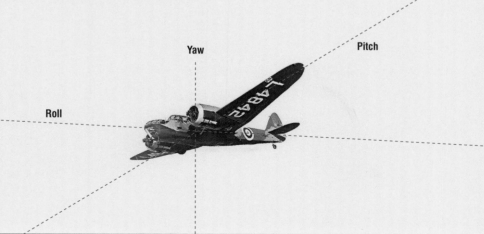

The axes cross at the aeroplane's centre of gravity. When the aeroplane is flying forward, it can rotate around the centre of gravity on each axis. On most aeroplanes, the pilot can control the movement using three flaps: the ailerons, the rudder and the elevators. When these change position, they change the flow of the air around the aeroplane. By changing the flow of air, the direction in which the aeroplane flies is also changed.

ROLLING is controlled by the ailerons on the wings. When the one on the left wing is up, the right one is down and the aeroplane rolls to the left. When the right one is up, the left one is down and the aeroplane rolls to the right.

YAWING is controlled by the rudder on the tail fin. When it moves to the left, the nose of the aeroplane goes left. When it moves to the right, the nose of the aeroplane goes right.

PITCHING is controlled by the elevators on the tail plane. When they are up, the tail of the aeroplane goes down, the nose goes up and it starts to climb. When they are down, the tail goes up, the nose goes down and the aeroplane starts to dive.

The WRIGHT BROTHERS story

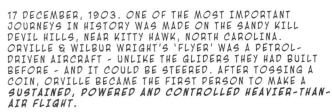

17 DECEMBER, 1903. ONE OF THE MOST IMPORTANT JOURNEYS IN HISTORY WAS MADE ON THE SANDY KILL DEVIL HILLS, NEAR KITTY HAWK, NORTH CAROLINA. ORVILLE & WILBUR WRIGHT'S 'FLYER' WAS A PETROL-DRIVEN AIRCRAFT - UNLIKE THE GLIDERS THEY HAD BUILT BEFORE - AND IT COULD BE STEERED. AFTER TOSSING A COIN, ORVILLE BECAME THE FIRST PERSON TO MAKE A *SUSTAINED, POWERED AND CONTROLLED HEAVIER-THAN-AIR FLIGHT.*

THE WRIGHT BROTHERS' EARLY EXPERIMENTS WERE PARTLY FINANCED BY INCOME FROM THEIR BICYCLE REPAIR SHOP IN DAYTON, OHIO. THEY MOVED OUT TO KITTY HAWK FOR ITS SAND HILLS WHICH WERE THE PERFECT PLACE TO LAUNCH TEST FLIGHTS. THEY TRIED OUT DIFFERENT CONTROLS AND WING SHAPES AND BUILT A PETROL ENGINE OF THEIR OWN DESIGN WHICH WAS LIGHTER THAN EXISTING MOTORS BUT STILL PROVIDED ENOUGH HORSEPOWER.

BICYCLE CHAINS CONNECTED THE FLYER'S LITTLE ENGINE TO TWO REAR-FACING PROPELLERS. THE 12M WINGS WERE 'WARPED' OR TWISTED BY WIRES AND THE ELEVATOR FLAPS AT THE FRONT, WHICH KEPT THE NOSE LEVEL, WERE CONTROLLED BY LEVERS. THIS IS HOW THE PILOT WAS ABLE TO CONTROL THE AIRCRAFT'S MOVEMENT.

THE WORLD STRUGGLED TO BELIEVE OR EVEN UNDERSTAND WHAT WILBUR AND ORVILLE HAD ACHIEVED, BUT BY 1908 THEY WERE ABLE TO TAKE AN IMPROVED AND MORE EFFICIENT FLYER TO EUROPE, WHERE FRENCH AVIATOR LOUIS BLERIOT USED THEIR 'WING-WARPING' TECHNIQUE TO CROSS THE ENGLISH CHANNEL.

THE BROTHERS SOLD THE FLYER DESIGN TO THE US ARMY AND TO MANUFACTURERS IN FRANCE. THEY RECEIVED THE GOLD MEDAL OF THE AERO SOCIETY OF GREAT BRITAIN AND INSPIRED CHARLES ROLLS AND GEORGE WHITE. SADLY WILBUR DIED AT THE HEIGHT OF THEIR SUCCESS. ONLY ORVILLE LIVED LONG ENOUGH TO SEE HOW SIGNIFICANTLY THEIR INVENTION WOULD CHANGE THE 20TH CENTURY.

ROLL UP, ROLL UP, LADIES & GENTLEMEN, I'LL TELL YOU 'BOUT THE BRAVEST, CLEVEREST, *DARING*-EST FLYING COWBOY THE WORLD'S EVER SEEN!

SAMUEL F CODY'S THE NAME! THE '*F*' STANDS FOR '*FIRST**', AS IN *FIRST FELLER IN BRITAIN TO BUILD AND FLY AN AEROPLANE!* THAT'S RIGHT FOLKS, I'M A GENUINE *AVIATION PIONEER!*

* NOT TRUE, IT STANDS FOR FRANKLIN. (-ED.)

I WAS BORN IN TEXAS** BACK IN 1861. MY PA WAS THE ONE AND ONLY *BUFFALO BILL CODY***, SO YOU MIGHT SAY THE WILD WEST WAS IN MY *BLOOD.*

AS A YOUNGSTER I WORKED AS A COWBOY AND A *BRONCO BUSTER* - THAT'S A FELLER WHO TAMES WILD HORSES. OUT ON THE CATTLE TRAILS I MET SOME CHINESE FOLKS WHO INTRODUCED ME TO *KITE-FLYING.* THAT'S HOW MY INTEREST IN AVIATION GOT STARTED.

** NOT TRUE EITHER, HE WAS BORN IN IOWA.
*** SO NOT TRUE THAT BUFFALO BILL SUED HIM!

IN THE 1880S I TURNED MY RIDIN', SHOOTIN' AND LASSOIN' SKILLS INTO A SPECTACULAR *STAGE SHOW* WHICH TOOK ME ALL OVER THE WORLD. MY WILD WEST ANTICS WERE A BIG HIT IN BRITAIN AND I MADE A PILE OF MONEY. I DECIDED TO GET INTO THE *FLYING* GAME.

I REMEMBERED THOSE CHINESE KITES AND FIGURED IF THEY WERE MADE BIG ENOUGH THEY MIGHT LIFT FOLKS RIGHT OFF THE GROUND. IN 1901 I PATENTED A *MAN-CARRYING KITE!*

THE BRITISH ARMY GOT INTERESTED AND IT WASN'T LONG 'FORE I WAS THEIR *CHIEF KITE INSTRUCTOR.* NOW, YOU MIGHT BE WOND'RING WHY SOLDIERS WANT TO PLAY WITH KITES - FACT IS THEY'RE PERFECT FOR OBSERVATION AND RECONNAISSANCE.

I NEARLY GOT KILLED IN A KITE ONE TIME - SOME LAME-BRAINED NAVY CAPTAIN FORGOT HE WAS TOWING ME AND TURNED HIS SHIP AROUND!

BUT MOSTLY ME AND THE BRITISH MILITARY GOT ON FINE. WE DID SOME PRETTY GOOD WORK TOGETHER, LIKE THE *NULLI SECUNDUS*, BRITAIN'S FIRST EVER *DIRIGIBLE.* I DIDN'T DESIGN HER, BUT THE ENGINE SECTION WAS PRETTY MUCH ALL MINE AND IT WAS ME WHO FLEW HER OVER LONDON IN 1907!

... AND THEN THERE WAS THE *BRITISH ARMY AEROPLANE NUMBER ONE*, A.K.A. 'THE FLYING CATHEDRAL'. THAT'S WHEN I BECAME THE FIRST IN BRITAIN TO BUILD AND FLY A PLANE, BACK IN '08...

THE ARMY BOUGHT TWO OF MY *BIPLANES* IN 1912. SOME FOLKS SAY MINE WEREN'T THE *BEST* AIRCRAFT IN THE TRIALS AND ONLY BEAT THE OTHER CONTENDERS 'CAUSE I WAS THE BEST PILOT! IT'S TRUE THAT WITHOUT ME IN THE HOTSEAT BOTH PLANES SOON CRASHED, BUT IT'S LIKE I ALWAYS SAY, 'FLYIN'S A DANGEROUS BUSINESS - TRY THE CODY ANTI-CONCUSSION HELMET!'

IT WAS MIGHTY HARD GETTING THE ARMY TO PAY ME. LUCKILY, THERE WAS PLENTY OF MONEY IN *AERO CONTESTS.* I ENDED UP TAKING BRITISH CITIZENSHIP SO I'D BE QUALIFIED TO COMPETE FOR THOSE FAT CASH PRIZES.

IN 1913 I WAS GEARING UP FOR A BIG CONTEST. HAD ME A NICE *SEAPLANE*, BUT I TRIED HER OUT ONE TIME AND SHE JUST BROKE UP UNDER ME. AT 500 FEET! ME AND MY UNFORTUNATE PASSENGER DROPPED LIKE *STONES.*

WELL, THAT MIGHT'VE BEEN THE END OF SAM CODY *THE MAN*, BUT THERE WAS NO STOPPING *THE LEGEND!* 50,000 PEOPLE SHOWED UP AT THE FUNERAL, EVEN THE KING SENT A TELEGRAM!

NOWADAYS FOLKS REMEMBER ME FOR MY PIONEERING WORK WITH *KITES* AND FOR MY WILD WEST *SHOWMANSHIP* WHICH MADE AVIATION A BIT MORE COLOURFUL. THAT '*F*' IN SAMUEL F CODY? STANDS FOR FLAIR, FEARLESSNESS AND FLAMBOYANCE!

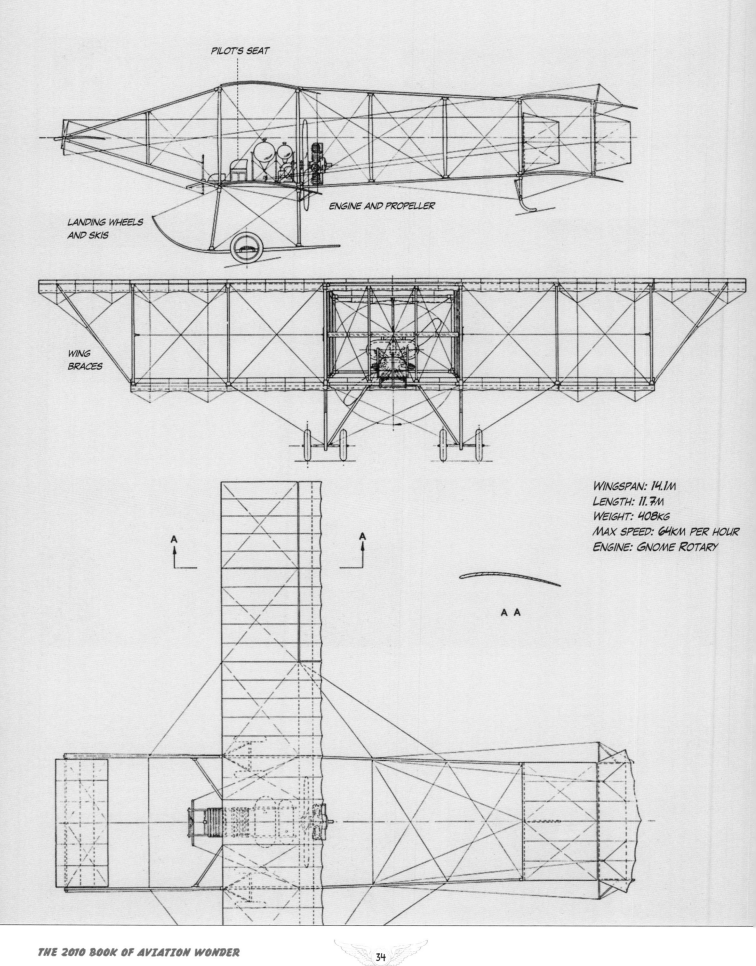

PILOT'S SEAT

ENGINE AND PROPELLER

LANDING WHEELS
AND SKIS

WING
BRACES

A   A

A A

WINGSPAN: 14.1M
LENGTH: 11.7M
WEIGHT: 408KG
MAX SPEED: 64KM PER HOUR
ENGINE: GNOME ROTARY

M. Tetard in Flight on Durdham Downs

A picture by David Gentleman from the book *Bristol Fashion* showing a Boxkite being used for army exercises on Salisbury Plain (left)
(REPRODUCED BY PERMISSION OF THE ARTIST).

A Boxkite flying over the Bristol Downs, November 1910 (above)
(PRIVATE COLLECTION).

BRISTOL BOXKITE

THIS WAS THE FIRST SUCCESSFUL AEROPLANE BUILT BY THE BRITISH & COLONIAL AEROPLANE COMPANY AT FILTON. THE DESIGN WAS BASED ON THE FARMAN BIPLANE FROM FRANCE.

It is known as a biplane because it has two sets of wings, one above the other ('bi' means 'two' in Latin). The Boxkite made its first flight on 30 July 1910 at Larkhill near Salisbury Plain in Wiltshire. Eight Boxkites were ordered by the Russians in November that year, so this was also the first British aeroplane to be exported. The frame was made from wood. The top set of wings was connected to the lower set by wires and wooden struts. This kept them firm and strong – another word to describe this is 'braced'. There was no cockpit for the pilot. He had to sit out in the open.

LEARNING TO FLY

(photographed by T L Fuller, 1912 © J T Fuller)

Imagine what it must feel like to have your first flying lesson. It would probably be a mixture of excitement and fear. Now imagine how much more exciting and scary it must have been in the very early days of flight. You'd be taught by someone who'd only just learnt to fly himself and you'd be flying an aeroplane that had only just been built. You couldn't be certain it would actually get off the ground. You also couldn't be 100 per cent sure that a wing or part of the tail wouldn't fall to bits while you were up in the air. This is a picture of the flying school that Sir George White set up at Larkhill in Wiltshire. Some of the pupils in the picture had come all the way from Turkey and Australia to learn to fly there.

LABYRINTH

KING MINOS HAS ORDERED **DAEDALUS** TO GIVE HIS LABYRINTH A SPRING CLEAN. NOW HE HAS FINISHED AND HE WANTS TO GO HOME, TO WORK ON HIS NEW FLYING MACHINE. UNFORTUNATELY, THE DREADED **MINOTAUR** IS GUARDING THE EXIT!

DAEDALUS THOUGHT THIS MIGHT HAPPEN AND HE PLANNED AHEAD. WHEN HE BUILT THE LABYRINTH HE SECRETLY HID A **BRISTOL SYCAMORE** HELICOPTER, RIGHT IN THE CENTRE OF THE MAZE.

CAN YOU HELP DAEDALUS FIND HIS WAY TO THE HELIPAD?

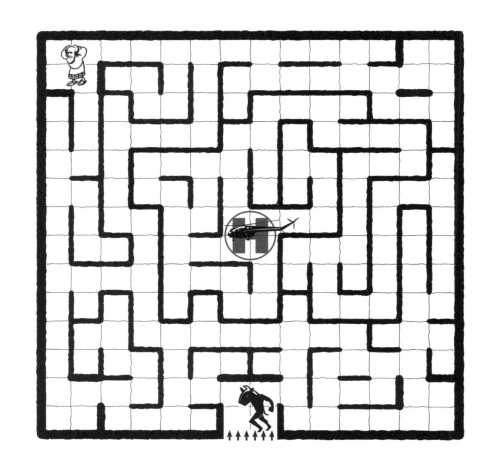

WORD PUZZLE

Rearrange these letters to spell the names of people who were involved in early flight. They've all been mentioned in this book already.

1. BILWUR THGWRI

2. RIHEN ANADCO

3. HARCLES SLLRO

4. RGEGEO LAYECY

5. DAUM OKCO

6. MAUESL YDOC

7. GGEEOR ITEHW

8. VILLOER RHWITG

9. CKRITPA XDERANELA

10. ZOENCNIV UNRDIAL

WORLD WAR ONE

LIKE MOST WARS, THE REASON THE FIRST WORLD WAR STARTED IN 1914 CAN SEEM VERY COMPLICATED. IT CAN ALSO SEEM VERY SIMPLE. IT WAS FOUGHT BECAUSE ONE GROUP OF COUNTRIES WANTED TO BE MORE POWERFUL THAN ANOTHER GROUP OF COUNTRIES. ON ONE SIDE WERE THE GERMAN EMPIRE, AUSTRIA-HUNGARY AND THE OTTOMAN EMPIRE. ON THE OTHER SIDE WERE THE EMPIRES OF BRITAIN, FRANCE AND RUSSIA. THIS SIDE WAS JOINED BY THE AMERICANS IN 1917. SOME OTHER COUNTRIES WERE ALSO INVOLVED BUT THESE WERE THE MAIN ONES.

Of course, it wasn't called the First World War or World War One then. Until 1939 when the Second World War started it was called the Great War. It was also sometimes called The War to End All Wars by the governments who were responsible for it. They were wrong about that.

Thousands of young men and many women volunteered to join the war effort. Most of them were expecting adventure and glory but they were in for a nasty shock. This was one of the last old wars and one of the first modern ones. Horses and riders were sent charging towards machine guns which cut them to pieces. Other terrible new weapons included mustard gas, tanks, flame-throwers and more powerful explosive shells than had ever been used before. When the war ended on 11 November 1918, many areas of Europe were in ruins. It is thought that 16 million people died because of the war, and 21 million were injured.

This was one of the first wars to use aeroplanes. In the beginning they were mainly used for observation – you could get a great view of the battlefield and the position of the armies from up there. But they were soon also dropping bombs on the soldiers in the trenches below and using their machine guns in aerial fights with enemy aircraft. It was dangerous work. The pilots flew in flimsy aircraft that were easily damaged and they usually didn't have parachutes to help them escape if they got into trouble. They often only had a few hours of training before they were sent off to fight. The average time a pilot served in the British Royal Flying Corps before he was shot down and killed was less than a month.

However, it was also a brilliant way to learn how to fly – providing you survived. Civilian life could seem a bit dull after the thrills of aerial combat, so after the war some pilots tried their luck as stunt fliers, entertaining the crowds at air shows by wing-walking, flying under bridges and looping-the-loop.

British airmen about to go into combat in a Bristol Fighter in the First World War (BRISTOL AERO COLLECTION).

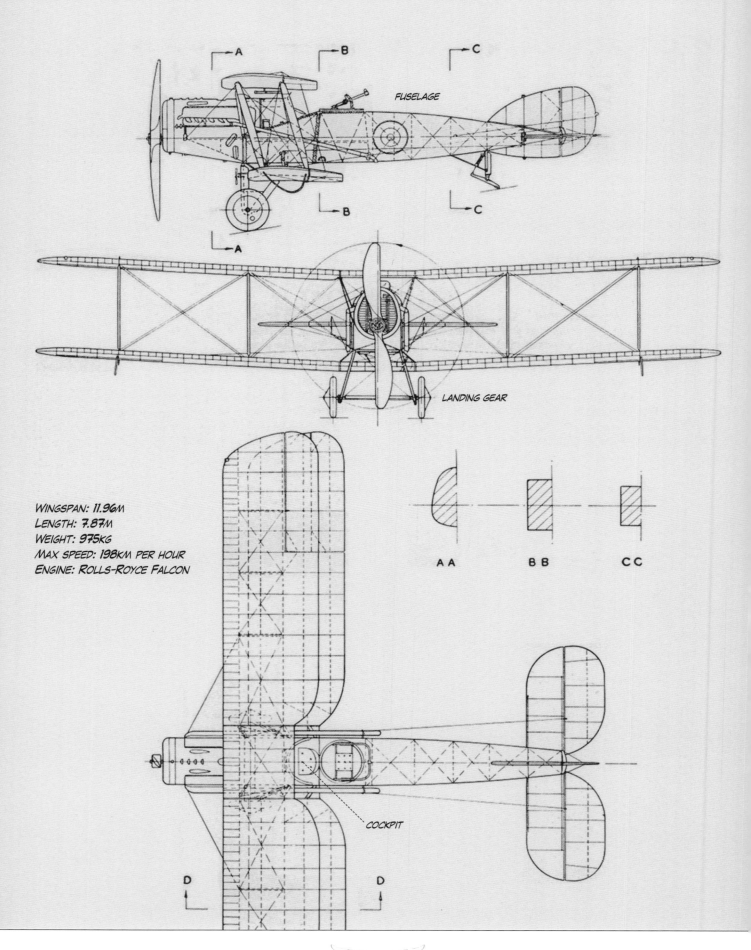

FUSELAGE

LANDING GEAR

WINGSPAN: 11.96M
LENGTH: 7.87M
WEIGHT: 975KG
MAX SPEED: 198KM PER HOUR
ENGINE: ROLLS-ROYCE FALCON

A A   B B   C C

COCKPIT

Fighter in action (above)
(BRISTOL AERO COLLECTION).

A vintage Fighter flying with a Tornado at an
airshow in the 1990s (above, right)
(BRISTOL AERO COLLECTION).

Doping wings (right) (BRISTOL'S MUSEUMS,
GALLERIES AND ARCHIVES).

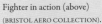

BRISTOL FIGHTER

THE BRISTOL FIGHTER WAS USED IN WORLD WAR ONE. IT
CARRIED A PILOT AND AN OBSERVER. WHEN THEY WERE
FIGHTING ENEMY AIRCRAFT, THE PILOT COULD FIRE A
MACHINE GUN THROUGH THE PROPELLER AT THE FRONT
OF THE AEROPLANE, WHILE THE OBSERVER COULD FIRE
ANOTHER GUN FROM THE BACK. THE OBSERVER COULD
ALSO DROP BOMBS.

By 1919 over 4,700 Fighters had been built for the British & Colonial
Aeroplane Company. Like the Boxkite, the frame of this biplane was made
from wood. The wings and fuselage (body) were covered in fabric which
was painted with a substance called dope. The dope made the material
tight so there was a smooth, aerodynamic surface. It also helped to keep
out water. This work was usually done by women who started working in
the factory when the men went to the war.

WONDERFUL WORLD OF
WINGS

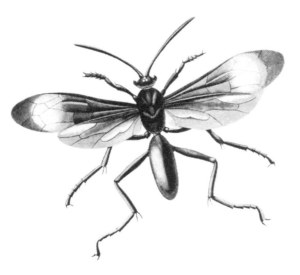

Wings provide the lift needed for flight. They also sometimes provide the thrust. The wings of insects are soft and light and covered in scales. These are the oldest natural wings in the world as they first evolved around 300 million years ago. Some insects – like the beetles – are pretty clumsy flyers, but others can perform amazing acrobatics in the sky. The midge has the fastest wing beat – 62,760 beats per minute.
(BATH IN TIME – BATH CENTRAL LIBRARY)

Pterosaurs are now extinct, but first appeared about 255 million years ago. The pterosaurs had light skeletons made from hollow bones, and triangular wings of skin. They were probably gliders rather than true flyers. (BRISTOL LIBRARIES)

Birds evolved about 150 million years ago. Like the pterosaurs, their skeletons are light. They have powerful muscles in their chests which give them the strength to beat their wings. On the downward stroke of the beat, the bird's wing moves forward, and the outer feathers twist to grasp the air ahead. This gives the bird thrust. The feathers on top of the wing give lift. The wing is curved like an aeroplane's wing. The word 'aviation', which is used to describe things to do with flight, comes from the Latin for bird, 'avis'. (UNIVERSITY OF BRISTOL LIBRARY, SPECIAL COLLECTIONS)

Bats first appeared about 55 million years ago. The bat's wing is a stretchy membrane and has over 20 different joints. It usually runs from the bat's shoulder to its ankle and stretches across its arm and hand bones. Bats can be more agile flyers than birds because their wings are more flexible.

When an aeroplane is flying, air is passing over and under its wings. The shape of an aeroplane's wing is called an aerofoil.

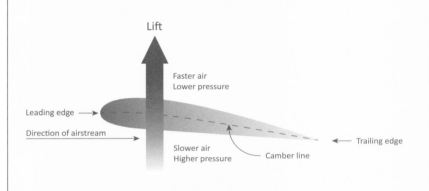

A typical monoplane aerofoil section.

The air pushed over the top of the wing is moving faster than the air below so is spread out more thinly. This creates lower air pressure above the wing than below. The curve of the aerofoil increases the speed at which the air flows.

It is the difference in pressure above and below the wing which gives the lift force keeping the aeroplane up. The speed of the air flow and the angle of the wing create the pressure difference. If the pilot flies too slowly there will not be enough lift. The wing will 'stall' and the aeroplane will drop. If this happens too close to the ground the aeroplane might crash, so pilots watch their speed very carefully.

The Braemar Bomber was a triplane built at the end of World War One by the British & Colonial Aeroplane Company. It had three sets of wings ('tri' means 'three'). The extra wings gave more lift so that heavy aeroplanes could fly at low speeds without stalling. They could also take off and land at small airfields with short runways. The struts and wires used to brace biplane and triplane wings gave a strong, light structure but increased the drag. (BRISTOL AERO COLLECTION)

The Racer was a monoplane built by the Bristol Aeroplane Company in the 1920s. Monoplanes without bracing struts are more aerodynamic and can fly faster than aeroplanes that have more than one set of wings. If they fly at lower speeds they need less thrust. That means they burn less fuel. But large monoplanes need longer runways for take-off and landing as they have less lift. In the early days several monoplanes broke up in the air and the British Army and Navy thought biplanes were safer. (BRISTOL AERO COLLECTION)

Gliders do not have thrust because they don't have engines but they do have lift to keep them airborne. They ride upon thermals – currents of warm air rising up from the ground. They gain height from one thermal and then glide down to the next one, losing height on the way. They can also gain height from the waves of air rising over hill tops. (ISTOCKPHOTO)

This is a Vulcan bomber powered by four Bristol Olympus engines. Like Concorde it has what is known as delta wings. That means they are triangular. Delta wings can be unstable at low speeds but they are very efficient at high ones. (ROLLS-ROYCE PLC)

The A350 is a new passenger aeroplane that is being developed by Airbus. It will have the largest wing ever produced for a single-deck, wide-body aircraft. (AIRBUS)

FASCINATING FACT

Scientists have found that dolphins are able to use their flippers like delta wings. The way dolphins move through water is similar to the way birds move through air. Their flippers give them lift and reduce drag, allowing the dolphins to swim at up to 20 miles an hour.

ACTIVITY!

When an open parachute falls through the air, gravity pulls it towards the ground. When something moves through the air there is always air pushing against it in the opposite direction.

This is called air resistance. Air is pushing up against the parachute and is trapped underneath it. This gives the parachute some lift. The lift isn't usually strong enough to keep the parachute up in the air, but it reduces the speed at which it falls so the parachutist can land safely.

MAKE A PARACHUTE

FASCINATING FACT

Jordaki Kuparento, a Polish aeronaut, was the first person to use a parachute to escape an aerial disaster. On July 24 1808 he ascended from Warsaw in a balloon, which caught fire. He jumped out, using his parachute to land safely.

Sticking the tape to the corners.

MATERIALS: square sheet of soft, pliable plastic; sticky tape; thin nylon twine; a cork.

EQUIPMENT: scissors.

1. Lay the sheet of plastic flat on the table.

2. Cut four pieces of twine that are twice as long as the sides of the sheet.

3. Attach one end of one of the pieces of the twine to one of the corners of the sheet using the sticky tape (see photo).

4. Repeat for the other three pieces and corners.

5. Attach the other ends of the pieces of twine to the cork. Make sure all the lengths of twine are the same length so the cork hangs down exactly in the centre of the parachute.

6. Raise your hand high in the air and let the parachute fall.

7. To test what difference the parachute makes, drop a cork on its own from one hand and your parachute from the other and see which one lands first.

WINGSPAN: 42.4M
LENGTH: 43.8M
WEIGHT: 70 TONNES
MAX SPEED: 780KM PER HOUR
ENGINE: EUROPROP INTERNATIONAL TP400-D

AIRBUS A400M

THE A400M IS A MILITARY TRANSPORT AEROPLANE. THE A400M WILL BE USED BY THE ROYAL AIR FORCE AND THE AIR FORCES OF OTHER EUROPEAN COUNTRIES.

Airbus A400M military transporter (main) (AIRBUS).

Engineer at Airbus, Filton working on the wings of an A400M (far left) (AIRBUS).

A400M wings being loaded for transport (left) (AIRBUS).

It is being assembled at the EADS factory in Spain. Its wings were designed at Airbus in Filton, where they are also built. The wings are made partly from carbon fibre-reinforced plastic. The wings on this aircraft are the largest in the world to be made from this type of composite material, which is very light and very strong. The more efficient a wing is in providing lift and reducing drag, the less fuel is needed to provide thrust. This saves energy and money, and helps reduce the damage to the environment.

SPOT THE DIFFERENCE

Look at this scene from *Brokelands*, a special airshow for flying ideas that never quite took off. There are **eight** differences between the two pictures, can you find them all?

WORD PUZZLE

Match each word to the correct definition. All the words have been used already in this book.

1. THERMAL
2. DOPE
3. AILERON
4. THRUST
5. STRUT
6. AERONAUT
7. PITCH
8. WEIGHT
9. RUDDER
10. AEROFOIL

A. CONTROLS ROLLING
B. DOWNWARD FORCE
C. TO DIVE OR CLIMB
D. CURRENT OF WARM AIR
E. SHAPE OF A WING
F. TYPE OF VARNISH
G. FORWARD FORCE
H. CONTROLS YAWING
I. PIECE OF WOOD USED TO BRACE WINGS
J. SOMEONE WHO FLIES

HOW **PISTON** ENGINES WORK

THE POWER OF A PISTON ENGINE IN AN AEROPLANE COMES FROM FOUR SEPARATE ACTIONS TAKING PLACE ONE AFTER THE OTHER INSIDE EACH OF THE ENGINE'S CYLINDERS.

AIR/FUEL INTAKE

☐ SUCK

The piston is pulled down, and air and fuel are sucked in through the inlet valve at the top of the cylinder.

■ SQUEEZE

The inlet valve closes, the piston is pushed up and the air inside the cylinder is squeezed (the technical word for this is 'compressed').

■ BANG

The fuel is set alight with a spark. This causes an explosion inside the cylinder (this is called 'combustion'). The piston is pushed down strongly. This provides the power to turn the aeroplane's propeller, which gives the aeroplane its thrust.

☐ BLOW

The exhaust valve opens at the top of the cylinder and hot gas from the explosion is pushed out. The exhaust valve closes, the piston is pushed up and the sequence begins again.

Four-stage diagram of piston cylinder (ROLLS-ROYCE PLC).

> **FASCINATING FACT**
> The output of a piston engine should be measured in Kilowatts, but people often use the old unit 'horsepower'. The inventor James Watt measured how much work a horse could do turning the wheels in a mill. This became his unit of measure, so if he said his engine produced 2hp it meant it could do the work of two mill horses. Watt quoted 'horsepower' so his customers would realise how many horses his engines could replace.

COMPRESSION

COMBUSTION
Intermittent

A piston engine is a type of internal combustion engine. Remember, that was what Cayley realised aeroplanes needed back in the early nineteenth century when engines were still being powered by steam.

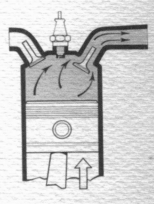

EXHAUST
Waste gases

PISTON ENGINES

PISTON ENGINES WERE FIRST USED IN CARS AND
MOTORCYCLES. SOME OF THE FIRST AEROPLANE
DESIGNERS TRIED USING THESE ENGINES IN THEIR
AIRCRAFT BUT THEY WERE EITHER NOT POWERFUL
ENOUGH OR TOO HEAVY TO FLY. ENGINES ESPECIALLY
DESIGNED FOR AEROPLANES WERE NEEDED.

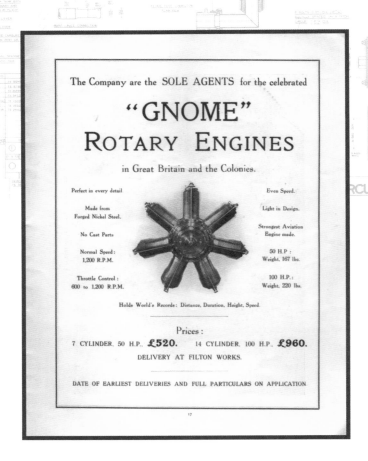

This is an advertisement for the Gnome rotary engine which was
used in the Bristol Boxkite. In the early aeroplanes there was a
danger that the engines would over-heat and burn out or even
set the aeroplane on fire (that wouldn't be much fun if you were
several hundred feet above the ground). The rotary engine had its
cylinders in a ring which rotated (spun round) at the same time as
the propeller turned. This helped prevent the engine overheating as
it was cooled by the cold air it was spinning through. (BRISTOL LIBRARIES)

This is the Falcon engine designed by Rolls-Royce in Derby which
was used in the Bristol Fighter. Its cylinders are in a line, rather
than in a circle, and are kept cool by the cold liquid that is pumped
around them. Many Falcons were built for Rolls-Royce by a firm in
Fishponds, Bristol called Brazil Straker. Their Chief Engineer was
Roy Fedden who designed the Jupiter engine you can see on the
next page. (ROLLS-ROYCE PLC)

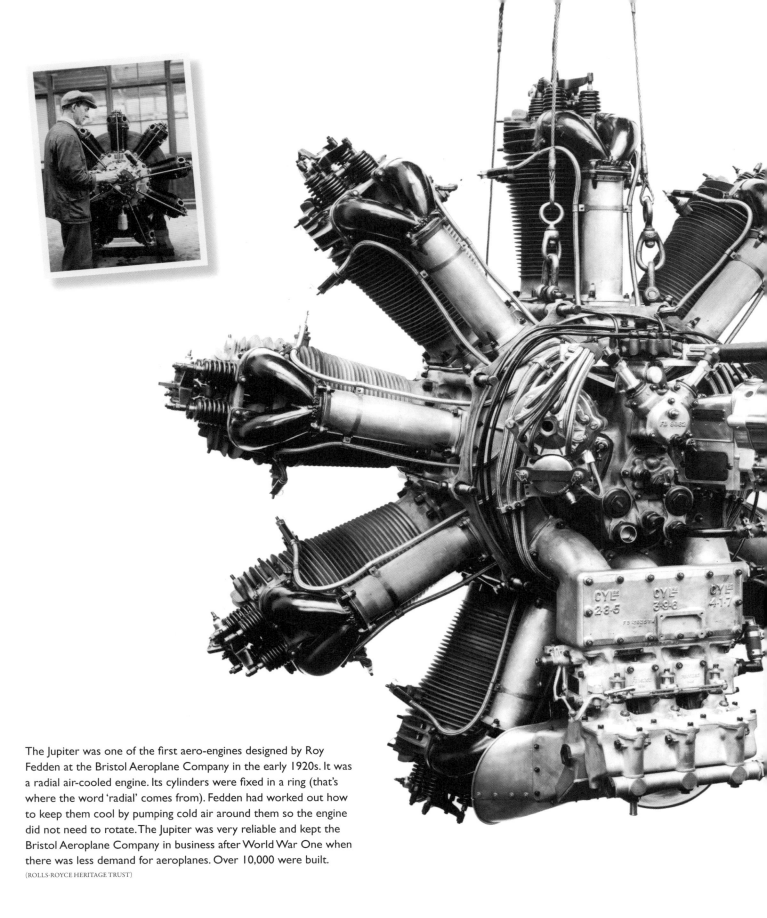

The Jupiter was one of the first aero-engines designed by Roy
Fedden at the Bristol Aeroplane Company in the early 1920s. It was
a radial air-cooled engine. Its cylinders were fixed in a ring (that's
where the word 'radial' comes from). Fedden had worked out how
to keep them cool by pumping cold air around them so the engine
did not need to rotate. The Jupiter was very reliable and kept the
Bristol Aeroplane Company in business after World War One when
there was less demand for aeroplanes. Over 10,000 were built.

PISTON ENGINES

This Hercules engine has 14 air-cooled cylinders arranged in two rows. Over 60,000 of these engines were built by the Bristol Aeroplane Company and they were used in 20 different types of aeroplane. This engine was designed in the late 1930s. A Hercules could go for 3,500 hours before it needed to be serviced (a Gnome engine had to be serviced every 20 hours). (ROLLS-ROYCE HERITAGE TRUST)

This is the Centaurus. This was the most powerful piston engine made by the Bristol Aeroplane Company. It was a two-row, 18-cylinder, air-cooled radial engine. About 8,000 of these were built. (ROLLS-ROYCE HERITAGE TRUST)

This woman is working on a milling machine that makes the pistons for Bristol engines. The picture was taken in the late 1940s. One and a half million pistons were made by the Bristol Aeroplane Company between 1932 and 1966. (ROLLS-ROYCE PLC)

PROPELLERS

All aeroplanes powered by piston engines use propellers. The propeller is turned using some of the energy produced by the BANG during the third stroke. The piston is connected to a crankshaft by a connecting rod. The power of the piston turns the crankshaft and the crankshaft turns the propeller. The amount of thrust the propeller provides depends on the speed at which it rotates and the angle (pitch) at which the blades cut through the air.

This is a two-blade propeller attached to a Bristol Jupiter engine in a Bullfinch monoplane. It was made in the early 1920s by the Bristol Aeroplane Company.
(ROLLS-ROYCE PLC)

This is a propeller workshop at the British & Colonial Aeroplane Company during World War One. Usually the propeller was made from laminated wood (layers of wood stuck together) rather than from a single, solid piece. Later propellers were made from aluminium.
(AIRBUS)

This picture shows a wing of the Bristol Beaufighter. It has a de Havilland three-bladed propeller fitted to a Bristol Hercules engine.
(ROLLS-ROYCE HERITAGE TRUST)

ACTIVITY!

When the propeller is rotated by the engine, it pushes the air around it backward. The air reacts to this by pushing the propeller forward. As the propeller is attached to the aeroplane, it pulls the aeroplane through the air.

MAKE A PROPELLER

MATERIALS: piece of card; cork; chopstick.

EQUIPMENT: scissors; knife.

1. Cut two blade shapes, 6cm long, from the card with the scissors. One end of each blade should be narrower than the other.

2. Cut the cork in half with the knife.

3. Push a hole through the cork with the chopstick to make a shaft.

4. Cut a slit on each side of the cork and glue the narrower ends of each blade in place (see picture).

5. Holding the chopstick lightly, blow on the propeller from the front and then from behind to see which way it turns.

6. Try twisting the blades slightly as this should improve the performance.

FASCINATING FACT

Aeroplane propellers were sometimes called airscrews. This word isn't used so much now because it's rumoured that someone ordered 20 airscrews and were sent 20 air-crews!

WORLD WAR TWO

THE SECOND WORLD WAR BEGAN IN SEPTEMBER 1939. IT IS ONE OF THE FEW WARS THAT ARE DESCRIBED AS 'A JUST WAR', ONE THAT <u>HAD</u> TO BE FOUGHT. THE NAZIS AND THE JAPANESE <u>HAD</u> TO BE STOPPED FROM CONQUERING THE WORLD OR THEY WOULD HAVE KILLED OR IMPRISONED MILLIONS OF PEOPLE.

The Germans and Japanese were supported by the Italians and some other countries. This group is usually called 'the Axis'. The countries of the British Empire and the British Commonwealth were fighting in a group that is usually referred to as 'the Allies'. This group included France, Greece, Poland, Norway, Holland and the Philippines. The Russians joined the Allies in 1941 when Germany attacked them without warning. The Americans also joined the Allies in 1941 after the Japanese bombed the US Navy at Pearl Harbour in Hawaii.

Aeroplanes played a much bigger part in the Second World War than they had in the First. Bombs could now reach far beyond the battle grounds where the armies were fighting as aeroplanes could travel much further. Many more bombs could be dropped as the aeroplanes were now much bigger so had more room to carry them. Engines were more powerful so they could carry the heavier loads.

Fighter aeroplanes were used to shoot down enemy bombers before they reached their targets. They also fought with each other in aerial 'dog fights' to gain control of the skies. The famous Battle of Britain, which took place from July to October 1940, was the world's first battle to be fought entirely in the air. Nearly 3,000 pilots fought on the side of the Allies. Over 500 of these were killed.

At first only military targets were attacked by the two sides. These were places that helped the war effort, like radar stations, airfields, ammunition factories and naval dockyards. In September 1940 the Bristol Aeroplane Company factories at Filton and Patchway were bombed by the Germans, who wanted to stop more aircraft and engines being built there. Around 150 people were killed and over 400 injured in this raid.

As the war went on, thousands of civilians also became targets of air raids as both sides bombed each other's towns and cities. This was either the result of poor aiming or was deliberate. Children had to be evacuated to the country to escape the danger. It was a frightening and confusing time for many people. But some also found it exciting and they liked the idea of standing up to the enemy and refusing to give in.

The war in Europe ended in May 1945 when the Allied armies reached Berlin and the Germans surrendered. The war with Japan ended in August 1945 after the Americans dropped atomic bombs on Hiroshima and Nagasaki. At least 61 million people are thought to have died because of the Second World War.

Bomb damage in Bristol after a night of attacks by the Germans (BRISTOL RECORD OFFICE).

SHOW TIME

LOOK AT THAT *HORRIBLE CLOUD!* NOT ONLY AM I GOING TO A *BORING AIR SHOW* — I'LL PROBABLY GET RAINED ON TOO!

THERE'S *NOTHING* BORING ABOUT AIR SHOWS, AMY. IN FACT —

WHOOOOOOOOSHH

SKREEEE!!!

WHAT WAS *THAT?!*

LOOK DAD! IT'S *ACTUALLY* LANDING ON THE ROAD!

DAD?

AIRBA

HEY! ARE YOU ALRIGHT IN THERE? ARE YOU HURT?

ABSOLUTELY FINE, DEAR! *TEENSY* GLITCH, NOTHING TO FRET ABOUT!

WHY ARE YOU FLYING THAT OLD-FASHIONED PLANE? ARE YOU IN THE AIR SHOW?

"AIR SHOW"? I SUPPOSE YOU *COULD* CALL IT THAT!

BUT THERE'S NOTHING OLD-FASHIONED ABOUT *THIS* LITTLE BEAUTY - SHE'S FRESH FROM THE FACTORY WITH A BRAND NEW *ROLLS-ROYCE* ENGINE... BETTER NOT SAY TOO MUCH — 'LOOSE LIPS SINK SHIPS'!

NEVER MIND SINKING SHIPS, YOU NEARLY *SQUASHED* OUR CAR!

AH, YES, SORRY ABOUT THAT. BLASTED NUISANCE REALLY. I'M AN 'ATA GIRL', YOU SEE. AIR TRANSPORT AUXILIARY? WE FERRY SPITFIRES AND SO ON FROM THE FACTORY TO THE RAF. THIS TIME I RAN INTO A PAIR OF BFS* - PERSISTENT BLIGHTERS WHO WOULDN'T BE SHAKEN OFF.

*BFS: MESSERSCHMITT BF 109E FIGHTER AIRCRAFT

THEY DON'T LET US ATAS HAVE GUNS, SO ALL I COULD DO WAS HEAD FOR CLOUD COVER.

TROUBLE IS, THEY DON'T GIVE US RADIO EITHER, OR NAVIGATION INSTRUMENTS, SO WHEN I CAME OUT OF THE CLOUD I WAS UTTERLY LOST - HAD TO MAKE AN UNSCHEDULED STOP TO CHECK THE DAMAGE AND GET MY BEARINGS.

I COULD GO AND GET DAD'S SAT NAV OUT OF THE CAR?

NO TIME, I'M AFRAID...

WE'VE GOT COMPANY!

WEMBLE AIR SHOW IS JUST UP THE ROAD. DOES THAT HELP?

WEMBLE? KNOW IT WELL! THANK YOU DEAR, JUST WHAT I NEEDED TO GET BACK ON COURSE!

MUST DASH! OR YOU'LL NEVER BE RID OF THESE TWO PESTS! TA RA!

"MEEE!! TFF!! TFF!

NEIN!

HIMMEL!

CATCH ME IF YOU CAN, BOYS!

AT WEMBLE AIR SHOW...

LADIES AND GENTLEMEN, WE'RE VERY SORRY BUT DUE TO APPROACHING HEAVY CLOUD, THERE WILL BE NO FURTHER DISPLAYS TODAY. WE -

GASP!

COME ON DAD, WE'RE MISSING THE AIR SHOW!

THE END

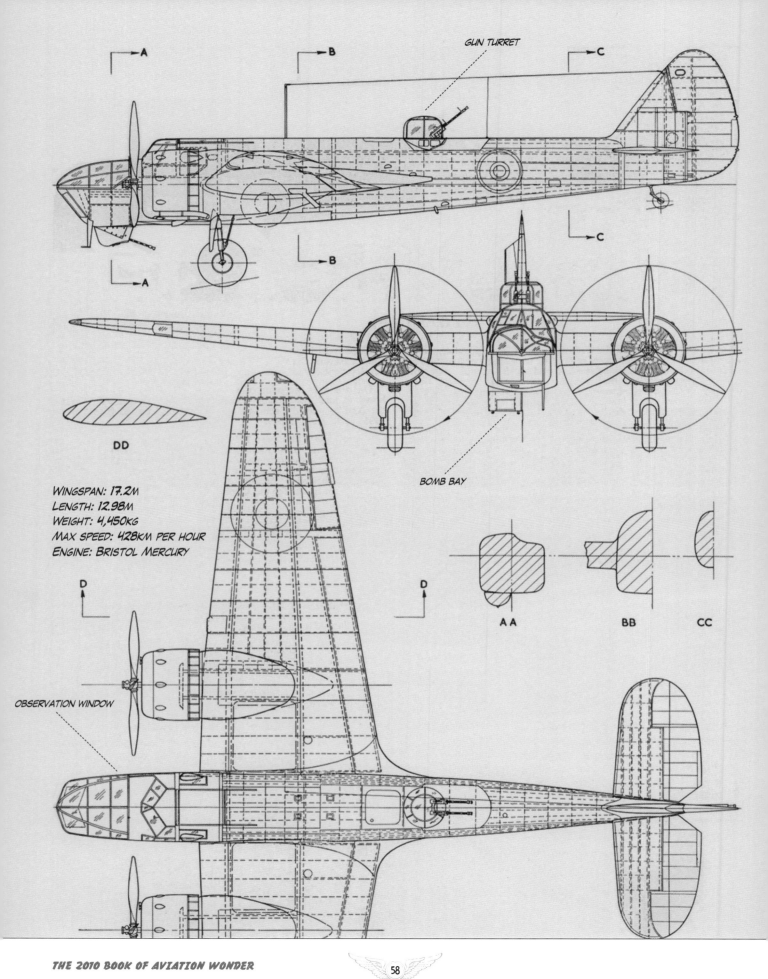

GUN TURRET

A

B

C

A

B

C

DD

WINGSPAN: 17.2M
LENGTH: 12.98M
WEIGHT: 4,450KG
MAX SPEED: 428KM PER HOUR
ENGINE: BRISTOL MERCURY

BOMB BAY

D

D

A A   BB   CC

OBSERVATION WINDOW

Women at work in the Bristol Aeroplane
Company during World War Two
(BRISTOL AERO COLLECTION).

BLENHEIM BOMBER

THE BLENHEIM WAS A BOMBER USED IN THE SECOND
WORLD WAR THAT WAS BUILT BY THE BRISTOL AEROPLANE
COMPANY. IT WAS WHAT IS KNOWN AS A STRESSED-SKIN
AIRCRAFT. IN THE OLDER AIRCRAFT, LIKE THE FIGHTER,
THE AEROPLANE'S WEIGHT WAS SUPPORTED BY A WOODEN
FRAME WHICH WAS COVERED BY FABRIC. IN THE BLENHEIM,
THE AEROPLANE'S WEIGHT WAS SUPPORTED BY ITS METAL
SKIN WHICH WAS RIVETED TO FRAMES AND STIFFENERS
UNDERNEATH.

Over 6,000 Blenheims were made. They were used by the Royal Air Force
and also sold to Finland, Romania, Portugal, Yugoslavia, Turkey, South
Africa and Egypt. A Blenheim dropped the first bombs for the Allies
at the start of the war. On that same day, a Blenheim was shot down and
its pilot was captured, making him the first British prisoner of war.
In 1943, when the Bristol Aeroplane Company was at its busiest, it
employed over 52,000 people. During the war it made over 14,000 aircraft
and 100,000 engines.

FILTON MADE MANY FAMOUS AIRCRAFT. THE MOST FAMOUS WERE THE BRISTOL BLENHEIM, AND THEN THE BRISTOL BEAUFIGHTER. OVER 6,000 'BEAUS' WERE MADE, FLYING IN COMBAT ALL OVER THE WORLD.

BEAUFIGHTER STORY

THE BEAU WAS SOMETIMES NICKNAMED 'WHISPERING DEATH' BECAUSE ITS ATTACKS WERE SO FAST AND SUDDEN.

PERHAPS THE MOST DARING EXPLOIT OF ANY BEAU WAS IN 1942 WHEN FLIGHT LIEUTENANT KEN GATWARD AND FLIGHT SERGEANT GEORGE FERN OF RAF COASTAL COMMAND FLEW ACROSS GERMAN-OCCUPIED FRANCE AT TREE-TOP LEVEL. THEY DROPPED A FRENCH TRICOLOUR FLAG IN THE MIDDLE OF PARIS, THEN SHOT UP THE LOCAL HQ OF THE GERMAN SECRET POLICE BEFORE SPEEDING SAFELY HOME AGAIN.

THAT'LL CHEER THE FRENCH UP A BIT!

RECORD BREAKERS

The aviation companies linked to George White and Charles Rolls have broken many records and achieved many firsts. Here are just a few.

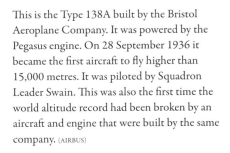

This is the nine-cylinder Pegasus engine made by the Bristol Aeroplane Company. The first aircraft to fly over Mount Everest were Westland biplanes that were powered by Pegasus engines. The flight took place in 1933. Pegasus engines also broke the world's distance record for aeroplanes in 1938. (ROLLS-ROYCE HERITAGE TRUST)

This is the Type 138A built by the Bristol Aeroplane Company. It was powered by the Pegasus engine. On 28 September 1936 it became the first aircraft to fly higher than 15,000 metres. It was piloted by Squadron Leader Swain. This was also the first time the world altitude record had been broken by an aircraft and engine that were built by the same company. (AIRBUS)

The Bristol Sycamore was the first all-British helicopter to be built. In the first picture its blades are folded back while it is on the ground. The second picture shows two of the Sycamores that were sold to the German air force in the 1950s. (BRISTOL AERO COLLECTION)

This shows a Bristol Proteus engine in the Bristol Britannia. The Britannia was the first passenger airliner to offer a scheduled non-stop service across the North Atlantic from London to New York. It also made the first non-stop airliner flight from New York to Vancouver, Canada. (ROLLS-ROYCE PLC)

HOW **JET ENGINES** WORK

LIKE THE PISTON ENGINE, THE JET ENGINE SUCKS, SQUEEZES, BANGS AND BLOWS. THE DIFFERENCE IS THAT THESE ACTIONS ARE TAKING PLACE CONTINUOUSLY IN DIFFERENT PARTS OF THE ENGINE. IF THE ENGINE CAN CONTINUOUSLY PRODUCE ENERGY IT CAN BE MORE POWERFUL AND EFFICIENT.

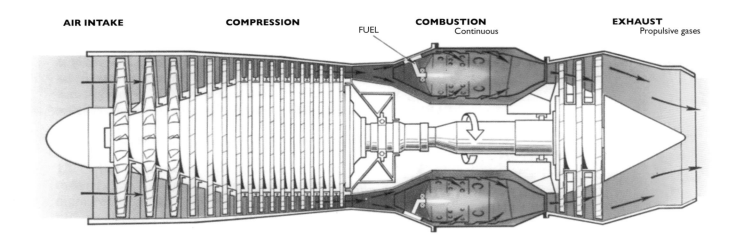

AIR INTAKE **COMPRESSION** FUEL **COMBUSTION** Continuous **EXHAUST** Propulsive gases

☐ SUCK

Air is sucked into the engine by the rotating blades at the front of the engine.

■ SQUEEZE

The air is driven through the engine by the compressor blades, which squeeze the air into a tighter and tighter space.

■ BANG

Fuel is sprayed into the compressed air and ignited so it bursts into flames.

☐ BLOW

The hot gases of the flames produce energy to turn the turbine blades. The turbine produces the power to drive the compressor. The gases blow out the back of the engine (the exhaust), thrusting the aeroplane forward.

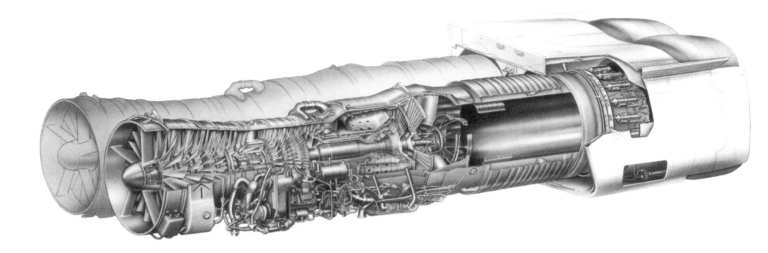

Above is an Olympus engine. It is a type of engine known as a turbojet. In a turbojet, all of the aeroplane's thrust comes from the jet of hot gas blown out the engine's exhaust. (ROLLS-ROYCE PLC)

Below is a Rolls-Royce RB211 Trent. It is a type of engine known as a turbofan. In a turbofan, the thrust comes from the jet of hot gas blown out the exhaust *and also* from the cold air that the huge fan at the front pushes around the sides of the core engine. An extra turbine is needed to drive the fan. All modern airliners are powered by turbofans, which can be quieter and cheaper to run than turbojets. (ROLLS-ROYCE PLC)

FASCINATING FACT

On 7 November 1945 a Gloster Meteor IV jet, built by the Gloster Aircraft Company, set a new world speed record by flying at 606 miles per hour. That was an amazing 137 miles per hour faster than the previous speed record. The Meteor was powered by Rolls-Royce Derwent engines made in Derby.

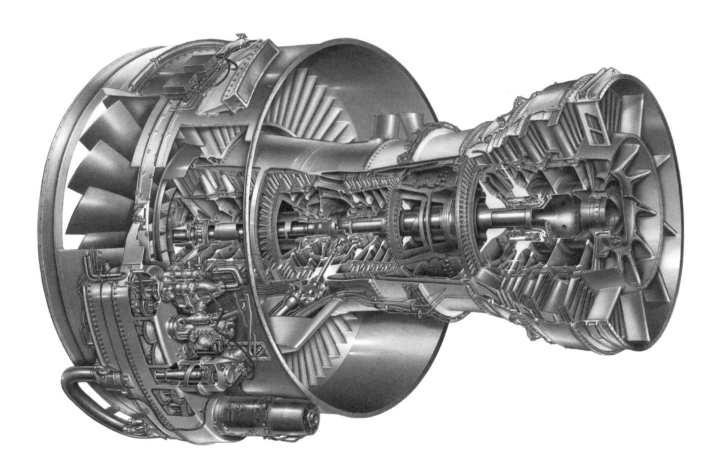

ACTIVITY!

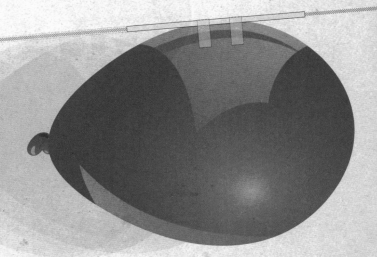

MAKE A BALLOON ROCKET

The thrust of a jet engine is a bit like when you let go of an unsealed balloon and the balloon whooshes away from you. Make a balloon rocket and you'll get an even better idea of how the jet engine works.

MATERIALS: thread; drinking straw; balloon; peg; sticky tape.

EQUIPMENT: balloon pump; scissors.

1. Attach a long length of thread to one side of the room.

2. Push the unattached end of the thread through a drinking straw.

3. Blow up the balloon so it's as big as it will go without bursting.

4. Twist the open end and hold it closed with a peg.

5. Use sticky tape to attach the balloon underneath the straw.

6. Pull the thread taut.

7. Undo the peg and watch the balloon whiz along the thread like a rocket.

Among the first people to sail west across the Atlantic were Bristol fishermen searching for new places where they could catch fish. This was way back in the fifteenth century. At that time Bristol was famous for making good, strong ships.

On May 20 1497 the explorer John Cabot set sail from Bristol across the Atlantic in his ship *Matthew*. He was looking for a route to Asia. Asia had gold, silk and spices – people could make their fortune there. The usual route was to go east by land and sea but this took a long time and there were many dangers. A lot of people thought it would be quicker and easier to go west – they already knew the earth was round but they didn't know that the continent of America was in the way. Cabot reached the large island that we now call Newfoundland on June 24 1497. He and his crew were probably the first Europeans to stand on the shore of North America.

Other important crossings of the Atlantic were made using Bristol ships. These included the voyages of the two steamships built in Bristol by Isambard Kingdom Brunel in the nineteenth century, PS *Great Western* and ss *Great Britain*.

The first aeroplane to cross from America to Britain was a Curtiss flying boat captained by the American pilot Albert Read. Read and his crew flew from Long Island, USA to Plymouth, England in May 1919. They had to do the journey in stages and it took them over 57 hours of flying time. The Atlantic crossing was from Newfoundland to Lisbon in Portugal with a stop at the Azores on the way.

The first non-stop flight across the Atlantic happened just a month later. British aviators John Alcock and Arthur Brown flew a Vickers Vimy biplane from Newfoundland to Ireland in June 1919. It was a dangerous journey. At one point, one of the instruments iced up because it was so cold and Brown had to climb out on the wing and chip the ice away. When they reached Ireland after a flight of 16 hours and 27 minutes they could see people waving at them from below. They thought they must be welcoming them so they waved cheerfully back. The people were actually warning them that they were headed for a bog instead of the landing field! They crashed and damaged the aeroplane but won a £10,000 prize for their successful flight. Their aeroplane was powered by a Rolls-Royce engine made at Derby – the Eagle VIII.

ATLANTIC CROSSINGS

Amelia Earhart standing in front of the Lockheed Electra in which she disappeared in 1937 (above) (SCIENCE AND SOCIETY PICTURE LIBRARY/NASA).

A replica of John Cabot's ship, *Matthew*, which you can sometimes see in Bristol's harbour (facing page, top) (DESTINATION BRISTOL: GRAHAM FLACK).

Alcock and Brown's biplane is on display in the Science Museum in London (facing page, bottom) (SCIENCE AND SOCIETY PICTURE LIBRARY/SCIENCE MUSEUM).

There was a third remarkable crossing of the Atlantic that year. It was by a Royal Air Force airship called R34 – also known as 'Tiny', even though it was *enormous*. It flew from Scotland to New York. There were two stowaways on board. Some of the crew had been told they must stay behind so the airship wouldn't be overloaded but one of them sneaked back on board, bringing with him a kitten called Whoopsie. The R34 landed in New York at 9.54am on 6 July after 108 hours 12 minutes of flying. The crew set off for the return journey three days later and arrived in London on 13 July.

In 1927 the American pilot Charles Lindbergh became the first person to fly solo across the Atlantic. He flew his monoplane The Spirit of St Louis from New York to Paris and won a prize of $25,000. The journey was 5,793km and took 33 hours 30 minutes. Lindbergh had to add extra fuel tanks to the aeroplane to get across the ocean. To help reduce the load, he wore special lightweight boots and sat in a chair made of wicker. There was no autopilot in those days so he had to keep awake and alert the whole time.

The next year Amelia Earhart became the first woman to cross the Atlantic in an aeroplane. She was the navigator on that flight but in 1932 she became the first woman to fly solo across the Atlantic. She flew from Newfoundland to Ireland in just under 15 hours. In 1937 she disappeared somewhere over the Pacific during a flight around the world. It is still a mystery what happened to her and her aeroplane.

CONCORDE

WINGSPAN: 25.6M
LENGTH: 61.66M
WEIGHT: 78.7 TONNES
MAX SPEED: 2,330KM PER HOUR
ENGINE: ROLLS-ROYCE/SNECMA OLYMPUS

Concorde seen from below front
(ISTOCKPHOTO).

SUPERSONIC FLIGHT

Supersonic aircraft are able to fly faster than the speed of sound. The speed of sound is about 1,226 kilometres per hour. It is often referred to by engineers as Mach 1 so any flight that is faster than Mach 1 is supersonic.

The Bristol Type 188 was a research aircraft built to study supersonic speeds. It first flew in April 1962. It was built at Filton. When the first factory was opened there by Sir George White, they were making aircraft from wood, wire and cloth. By the 1960s they were using stainless steel and flying at speeds Sir George could never have imagined.

When travelling at very high speeds, a huge amount of heat is generated around an aircraft. In the early 1960s it was thought that stainless steel would be the best material to cope with these very high temperatures.

The Type 188 did manage to make a short dash at around Mach 2 and the engineers learnt some useful things from studying the effect of extreme heat on the aircraft. However, it used much more fuel than was expected so the project was abandoned in 1964.

(BOTH PICTURES OF TYPE 188 FROM ROLLS-ROYCE HERITAGE TRUST)

The world's first supersonic airliner was Tupolev Tu-144, built by the Russians, which first flew in March 1968. However, the most famous supersonic airliner is Concorde. This was designed and built in a joint project by the British and French governments.

On 9 April 1969 the first British Concorde (Concorde 002) was flown from Filton for the first time. It was made from aluminium, which the engineers had decided was a much better material to use in high temperatures than stainless steel. During supersonic flights the airframe could stretch as much as 30 centimetres in the heat without being damaged.

Concorde's maximum speed was more than twice the speed of sound. It could fly people from London to New York in less than three and a half hours – that's about half the time it would take normal airliners. Because there is a five-hour time difference between the two cities, this meant that passengers arrived before they left!

Concorde was powered by Olympus engines which were built by Rolls-Royce and a French company called SNECMA.

Concordes flew passengers for British Airways from 1976 to 2003. The last Concorde to be assembled at Filton was Concorde 216, which was delivered to British Airways on 13 June 1980. On 26 November 2003 this aircraft made its final flight. You can now visit it at the Concorde Visitors Centre at Filton.

Chief Test Pilot Brian Trubshaw and Co-Pilot John Cochrane prepare for Concorde 002's first flight (top, left) (FILTON LIBRARY).

A British Airways Concorde takes off at Filton (top, right) (AIRBUS).

Concordes being assembled at Filton (above) (ROLLS-ROYCE PLC).

Now Concorde has been grounded, there are no longer any supersonic airliners flying. However, many military aircraft can fly at supersonic speeds. These include the Tornado and the Eurofighter Typhoon. The engines for these aircraft are designed and built by Rolls-Royce.

EJ200 engine (above, left) (ROLLS-ROYCE PLC).

Eurofighter Typhoon powered by EJ200 engines (above) (ROLLS-ROYCE PLC).

Tornado powered by RB199 engines (below) (ROLLS-ROYCE PLC).

BAGGAGE RECLAIM >>·>

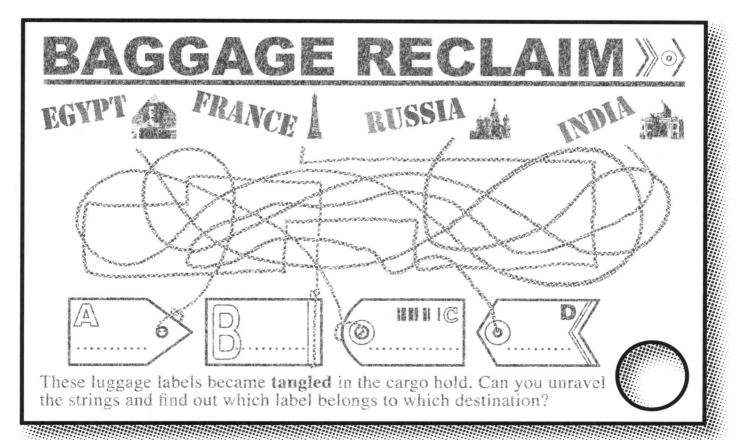

EGYPT FRANCE RUSSIA INDIA

These luggage labels became **tangled** in the cargo hold. Can you unravel the strings and find out which label belongs to which destination?

WORD PUZZLE

Match the names to the achievements. All have been mentioned already in the book.

1. SWAIN
2. LAROCHE
3. GIFFARD
4. MORANE
5. STRINGFELLOW
6. EARHART
7. CHAVEZ
8. FABRE
9. LILIENTHAL
10. LINDBERGH

A. FIRST TO FLY OVER THE SWISS ALPS.
B. BUILT FIRST MODEL AEROPLANE THAT FLEW.
C. FIRST PERSON TO FLY SOLO ACROSS ATLANTIC.
D. MADE FIRST HUMAN GLIDER FLIGHT.
E. BUILT FIRST POWERED AIRSHIP.
F. WORLD'S FIRST QUALIFIED FEMALE PILOT.
G. FIRST TO FLY HIGHER THAN 15,000 METRES.
H. FIRST TO FLY AT 100KM AN HOUR.
I. FIRST WOMAN TO FLY SOLO ACROSS ATLANTIC.
J. FLEW FIRST SEAPLANE.

PASSENGER TRAVEL

Passengers sit on wicker chairs in the elegant Bristol Pullman in 1920 (facing page) (BRISTOL'S MUSEUMS, GALLERIES AND ARCHIVES).

An advertisement for Imperial Airways from the 1930s. Imperial Airways owned the Empire flying boats and a fleet of airliners (below).

In the first years of heavier-than-air flight there wasn't much room for passengers. By the early 1920s bigger aeroplanes were being built as engines became more powerful and these could carry more people. However, it was often an uncomfortable ride. The passengers would usually have been squashed up together in hard chairs, unable to hear each other speak because of the noise.

This was before cabins were pressurised. The air inside the aeroplane was almost the same density and temperature as the air outside. The air gets thinner the higher you go and this can make you feel dizzy and sick because you're not getting enough oxygen when you breathe in. This meant the aeroplanes tried to keep fairly low in the sky. Because they were low down, there was more chance of getting knocked about by the thermals (remember them?) and by stormy weather. If the pilot decided to risk the altitude sickness and fly higher to avoid all the bumps, the passengers would not only have felt ill but would also have been shivering in their seats because there was no heating and it was very cold up there.

Some of these problems continued into the 1930s, but flying had become much more exciting by then because of the magnificent Empire flying boats. Flying boats could travel to distant, exotic places because, unlike ordinary aeroplanes, they didn't need a runway. They landed on and took off from water. Many of them were powered by Pegasus engines built by the Bristol Aeroplane Company. They were given the name 'Empire' because they carried passengers, mail and cargo around the British Empire, which at that time covered Canada, the Caribbean, parts of Africa, Asia and the Far East, Australia and New Zealand. The big flying boats could carry up to 20 passengers on day-time flights and around 12 on night ones when beds were used instead of seats.

The first modern passenger airliner was the Boeing 247. It was what is called 'state of the art' as it was so up-to-date – well, it was in 1933 and it still looks pretty modern. The Boeing 247 was a sleek, all-metal, twin-engined monoplane and one of the first to have an automatic pilot. It also had a sound-proofed cabin, an onboard toilet (very handy), and individual reading lights and air vents for each of its ten passengers. It could fly 50 per cent faster than any other airliner and in May 1933 set a new record by flying from New York to San Francisco in less than 20 hours.

Travel comfortably IMPERIAL AIRWAYS AND ASSOCIATED COMPANIES

Europe—Africa—India—China—Australia

Towards the end of World War Two the Bristol Aeroplane Company became involved in the Brabazon project. Does that name look familiar? Back in 1910 John Theodore Cuthbert Moore-Brabazon became the first qualified British pilot. He was later made Lord Brabazon of Tara and was in charge of a government committee that aimed to improve the British aircraft industry. The committee decided that one of the things Britain needed was a large airliner that could carry 100 passengers in comfort across the Atlantic. That was Brabazon, the biggest aeroplane ever built in Britain. The Brabazon was 54 metres long with a wingspan of 70 metres. It was so much bigger than other aeroplanes, that a special hangar had to be made for it at Filton and part of the village of Charlton had to be demolished to make room for its runway. In the end, no airlines wanted to buy it so it was scrapped in 1953.

The BAC had more luck with Britannia. This airliner made its first flight in 1952 and over 80 were built. Britannia was powered by the Bristol Proteus, a gas-turbine propeller engine, and gave such a smooth, quiet flight it was nicknamed the 'Whispering Giant'. It was used by airlines around the world including British Overseas Airways Corporation, Canadian Pacific and Air Spain.

By the 1950s jet engines were making passenger travel even more convenient. The jets were more powerful than the old piston engines. This meant airliners could be bigger and fly faster and further than before. Bigger airliners meant more passengers could travel, which meant cheaper tickets. Previously, airline passengers had generally been wealthy people who had the time and the money to take slow, expensive flights. Now more ordinary people could travel, though it was still a bit of a luxury.

The de Havilland Comet was the first jet to provide regular passenger services. It came into service in 1952 when it flew from London to Johannesburg. It was still fairly small – it carried around 40 passengers – but was twice as fast as most other airliners, flying at 500 miles an hour. Unfortunately, in 1954 two Comets exploded in mid-air as a result of metal fatigue so the fleet of Comets was grounded until the problem was solved.

Passenger jet travel really took off with the Boeing 707, which was first used by Pan American Airways for its New York to Paris service in 1958. The 707 could carry up to 180 passengers. The first wide-bodied 'jumbo' jet was the Boeing 747. It went into service in 1970 and could carry over 400 passengers. With these big American jets, air travel became even more affordable and more and more people in Britain began to take foreign holidays.

Different classes of passenger fares started to be used in the 1950s – up until then everybody travelled first class. The first new cheaper fare rate was known as 'tourist class'. This was followed by the even cheaper – and more uncomfortable – economy class. Some airlines also introduced a deluxe class for those who wanted to feel extra special – and were able to pay for all those special services.

Today, companies like easyJet and Ryanair provide really cheap air fares for passengers – they are even cheaper if you can book early. These are called 'no frills' airlines. There's only limited service on board and you have to pay extra for things which are usually included in a ticket price, like putting luggage in the hold and having something to eat.

The good thing about all these changes to passenger travel is that now even more people have the chance to see the world. It's also often cheaper and quicker to go by aeroplane than by train or car for quite short journeys too, like from Bristol or Cardiff to Glasgow. The bad thing about this is that when more people fly there is the risk of more damage being done to the environment.

FASCINATING FACT

The Comet was built by the de Havilland company. Geoffrey de Havilland learnt to fly in 1910 in an aeroplane he had designed and built himself. He loved nature and used to search for larks' nests near the airfield when he was testing his early aircraft so he wouldn't disturb them when he took off.

A Boeing 247 built in 1933. It became the oldest aircraft to have flown the Atlantic when it flew from Florida, USA to Wroughton in Wiltshire on 3 August 1983 (facing page) (SCIENCE AND SOCIETY PICTURE LIBRARY/SCIENCE MUSEUM).

Inside the Brabazon there was plenty of leg-room for the passengers but the aeroplane only went on test flights as no airline companies wanted to buy it (above) (BRISTOL AERO COLLECTION).

Picture from a brochure about the Britannia (right)
(BRISTOL AERO COLLECTION).

WINGSPAN: *79.8M*
LENGTH: *73M*
WEIGHT: *277 TONNES*
MAX SPEED: *1,020KM PER HOUR*
ENGINE: *ROLLS-ROYCE TRENT*

AIRBUS A380

THE A380 IS THE LARGEST PASSENGER AEROPLANE IN THE WORLD. ITS WINGS WERE DESIGNED BY AIRBUS AND ARE PARTLY BUILT BY GKN IN FILTON. IT MADE ITS FIRST COMMERCIAL FLIGHT ON 25 OCTOBER 2007 WHEN IT FLEW FROM SINGAPORE TO SYDNEY FOR SINGAPORE AIRLINES. IT CAN CARRY UP TO 525 PASSENGERS. IT HAS BEEN DESIGNED TO REDUCE THE ENVIRONMENTAL IMPACT OF FLYING BY USING MORE ENERGY-EFFICIENT MATERIALS, WINGS AND ENGINES.

Airbus A380 flying over Clifton Suspension Bridge (facing page) (AIRBUS).

A380 passengers (above) (AIRBUS).

Helicopters are more manoeuvrable than most other aircraft. They can fly in any direction – straight up, straight down, backwards and forwards – and also hover in one place.

Helicopters

A helicopter's rotor blades have an aerofoil shape so they are like spinning wings giving lift and thrust. In the early days of experiments in flight, many people thought that wings had to move, but the Wright brothers used fixed wings in their Flyer and so most designers stopped thinking about moving ones. However, the idea didn't die out completely. The first ever helicopter flight probably took place in 1907 when the Frenchman Paul Cornu managed to get airborne for about 20 seconds.

The autogyro is a forerunner of the modern helicopter (right). It was invented by the Spanish designer Juan De la Cierva in the 1920s. The autogyro has a propeller at the front which is powered by an engine. The propeller moves the autogyro forwards. The big rotor on top is only connected to the engine during take-off. Once the autogyro is airborne, the rotor no longer needs to use the engine to keep spinning. As long as it is moving forward, the airflow will turn it like a windmill and it will generate lift. The autogyro can climb and dive, but it can't hover. De la Cierva thought rotating wings were safer than fixed ones. As if to prove him right, he was killed in a fixed-wing aircraft which crashed on take-off.

One of the many advantages of having a helicopter is that it can get to difficult and dangerous places that aeroplanes and other vehicles can't reach. Because they can hover, helicopters can be used to rescue people on sea or land. It takes skill to keep the helicopter steady. The pilot has to make sure that the blades on the rotor are spinning at just the right angle, otherwise the helicopter might shoot away from the spot. On the right is a picture of a Bristol Sycamore taken in the 1950s during a practice rescue at sea. The Sycamore could quickly be converted for different uses: for rescue missions, as an air ambulance, as a passenger carrier and as an aerial crane. (BRISTOL AERO COLLECTION)

The Bristol Type 173 helicopter was the first twin-engine, twin-rotor aircraft built in Britain (above). It made its first successful hover in January 1952. (BRISTOL AERO COLLECTION)

Rolls-Royce at Filton makes the Gem engine that is used in the Lynx helicopter (right). Since 1986 the Gem has held the helicopter world speed record of just over 400km per hour. (ROLLS-ROYCE PLC)

FASCINATING FACT

Juan De la Cierva got his inspiration for rotating wings from nature. Some seeds, like the seeds of the sycamore and maple tree, are carried in pods shaped like a rotor blade or a propeller. Instead of falling straight down, they are caught up by thermals and spun round and round, so they travel away from the parent tree. This means they have a better chance of growing. (ISTOCKPHOTO)

MAKE
PAPER
AEROPLANES

There are lots of different ways to make a paper aeroplane. This is one of the best. It is the Dragon Paper Airplane by Alex Schultz. There's a video demonstration on the website www.paperairplanes.co.uk to help you follow the instructions. All you need is an A4 sheet of paper.

Diagram 1

Diagram 2

Diagram 3

Diagram 4

Diagram 5

Diagram 6

MATERIALS: A4 sheet of paper.

1. Fold down the centre of the paper, one long edge to the other long edge, then open the paper out again. Now fold along the diagonal dotted lines, as shown in **Diagram 1**, bringing the corners in so they touch the centre line.

2. Fold along the dotted diagonal lines shown in **Diagram 2**. The top left and top right edges must meet along the centre line.

3. Fold along the horizontal dotted line shown in **Diagram 3**. The tip of the paper aeroplane must touch the bottom of the paper. Make sure the tip is in the centre.

4. Fold along the diagonal dotted lines in **Diagram 4**. The left top edge and right top edge must meet at the centre line.

5. You should now have two pointed tips, one pointing down and one pointing up. Fold back the flap that is pointing down along the dotted line shown in **Diagram 5.** The tip of this flap must touch the tip pointing up. **This is very important**. If the tips do not meet go back and re-do the folding so that they do.

6. Fold back along the centre line again. Finally fold along the dotted lines shown in **Diagram 6** so the edges meet at the centre.

7. You should now have an aeroplane that looks like the photograph above and be ready to fly. Hold the aeroplane about ¼ of its length from the nose tip and throw it overarm using a straight, smooth throw. You can try creating ailerons to make your aeroplane roll by tearing the paper on the wings to make flaps. You can also try adding weights – like a blob of plasticine on the nose or paper clips on the wing tips – to see what difference that makes to its performance.

Ideas, materials and techniques that have come from designing and building aeroplanes can sometimes be used to make other things. This is called 'transferable technology'. People who have built aeroplanes can learn to make something different. They have 'transferable skills'.

From Aeroplanes to...

After World War Two there was a housing shortage because so many homes had been damaged or destroyed by bombing. There was also lots of left-over aluminium lying around that had been bought to build aeroplanes and was no longer needed. The Bristol Aeroplane Company put these two things together and decided to build aluminium bungalows to help the homeless (right). Large sections of the homes were made in the factory, taken by lorry to the building site and then quickly put together. This type of building is called a pre-fab, which is short for 'pre-fabricated' ('pre-made'). Aluminium is strong but light so it was the perfect material to use. The Bristol Aeroplane Company not only made pre-fab homes but also schools and other large buildings, some of which were packed up in crates and sent abroad. (BRISTOL AERO COLLECTION)

The
A·I·R·O·H
HOUSE
THE BRISTOL AEROPLANE COMPANY LIMITED

The Bristol Aeroplane Company began making high-quality cars after World War Two. Making cars and other products helped to keep the company's employees in work when there were fewer orders for aeroplanes. The car department became a separate company called Bristol Cars in 1960. They still make very expensive, luxurious cars today. This photo shows a Bristol 406 car next to Britannia outside the Brabazon hangar at Filton (left). (BRISTOL OWNERS' CLUB)

This photo was taken at the Bristol Aero Collection in Kemble where you can see an Alpha dinghy from the 1950s called Polly Esther (right). The Bristol Aeroplane Plastics Division made the hull of these dinghies, which were the first sailing boats to be made from fibre glass. The company started out making plastic fittings for aircraft, like the air conditioning tubes of the Britannia, but soon found other uses for this new material. Among the other things they made were bodies for sports cars, pipes for water wells and cases for bombs.
(BRISTOL AERO COLLECTION)

British Aerospace at Filton made aircraft, including Concorde, but the company was also involved in space projects. One of these was Giotto, which was designed to gather information about comets (below). It was known as a comet interceptor or probe. Giotto was launched in July 1985. In March the next year it caught up with Halley's comet. Film of the comet was watched live on television around the world. Giotto was also used to take the first colour photographs of the inside of a comet and gathered useful information about what the comet was made of.
(SCIENCE AND SOCIETY PICTURE LIBRARY/SCIENCE MUSEUM)

FROM AEROPLANES TO...

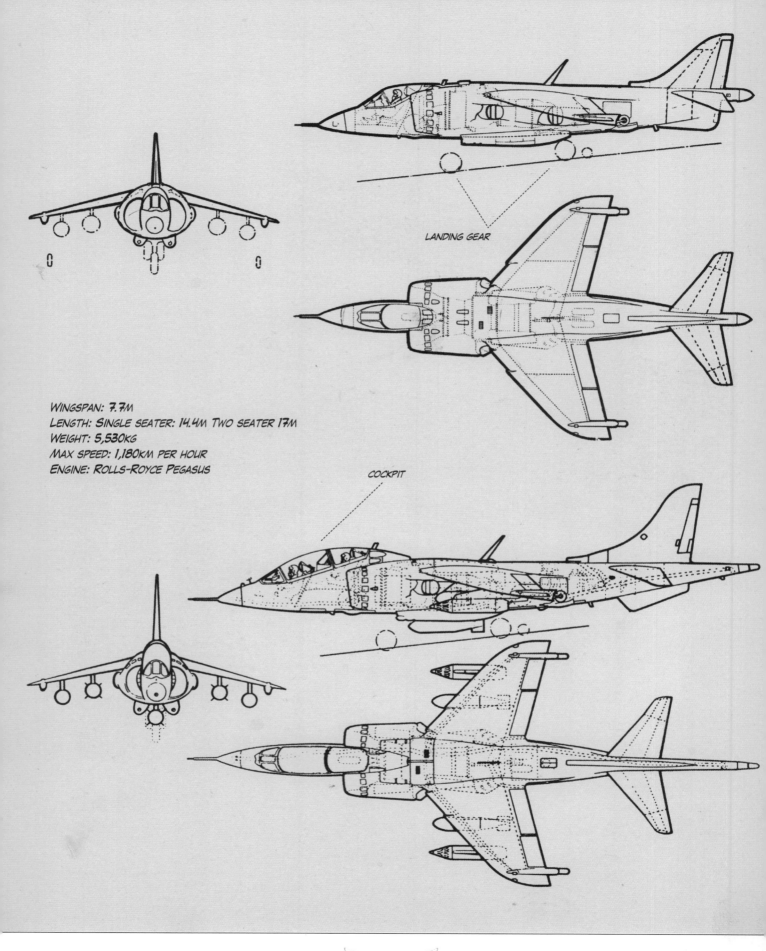

WINGSPAN: 7.7m
LENGTH: SINGLE SEATER: 14.4m TWO SEATER 17m
WEIGHT: 5,530kg
MAX SPEED: 1,180km PER HOUR
ENGINE: ROLLS-ROYCE PEGASUS

LANDING GEAR

COCKPIT

HARRIER

THE HARRIER JUMP JET WAS THE FIRST AEROPLANE CAPABLE OF VERTICAL OR SHORT TAKE-OFF AND LANDING (V/STOL) THAT WENT INTO SERVICE. GORDON LEWIS, A DESIGNER AT BRISTOL AERO ENGINES AT FILTON IN THE 1950S, HAD DEVELOPED AN IDEA OF FITTING ENGINES WITH NOZZLES THAT COULD SWIVEL ROUND. THIS MEANT THAT THEY COULD BE USED VERTICALLY - TO SEND THE AIRCRAFT STRAIGHT UP - OR HORIZONTALLY - LIKE A NORMAL JET.

The engine he designed for the Harrier is called Pegasus (this is a bit confusing as it has the same name as the piston engine you've seen before, but this is a turbofan). There are two pairs of nozzles on each engine. They can swivel through 98.5 degrees. The Harrier was first used by the Royal Air Force in the early 1970s. Versions of the Harrier are now also used by the Royal Navy, United States Marine Corps and Spanish Navy.

Harrier landing onto the deck of a ship (main image) (ROLLS-ROYCE PLC).

Inspecting the engine of a Harrier used by the Spanish Navy (above, left) (ROLLS-ROYCE PLC).

Here's an idea from the Bristol Aeroplane Company in the 1950s for a wingless aircraft that used swivelling engine nozzles to hover in the air. It was never built (above) (BRISTOL AERO COLLECTION).

BLOODHOUND

The Bloodhound was a surface-to-air missile that was developed by the Bristol Aeroplane Company after World War Two. It was designed to destroy enemy aircraft and missiles before they had a chance to do any damage of their own. When this type of defence was first being planned, many people in Britain were afraid of the countries behind what was then known as the Iron Curtain, the imaginary line that divided Europe into east and west. This period in history was known as the Cold War.

The Bloodhound was used by the Royal Air Force from 1958 until 1993. It was also used by the governments of Australia, Sweden, Switzerland and Singapore. It was launched using four booster rockets and then powered to its target by two Thor ramjet engines. A ramjet is smaller and simpler than other types of jet engines, but is just what is needed to send a high-speed missile through the air. Bloodhound could go from zero to 1,000 miles per hour in just two seconds.

The Bloodhound was 8.46 metres long and had a diameter of almost 55 centimetres. Its top speed was Mach 3. That's three times faster than the speed of sound. It could travel a distance of 185 kilometres.

Launch of a Bloodhound missile
(ROLLS-ROYCE HERITAGE TRUST).

"ENGINE WORDS"

The answers to these questions are all
PARTS OF ENGINES
or
ENGINE NAMES.

1 The gas-turbine propeller engine in the Britannia airliner.

2 The driving force behind the 600mph Gloster Meteor IV.

3 A 9-cylinder engine named after a mythical horse.

4 Radial engine designed by Roy Fedden at the Bristol Aeroplane Co.

5 The part of an engine which turns to drive the compressor.

6 The sequence of a piston engine: suck, _ _ _ _ _ _ _, bang, blow.

WORD PUZZLE

Which of the following statements do you know are true from reading this book?

TRUE	FALSE	
○	○	1. THE FIRST BRITISH AEROPLANE TO BE EXPORTED WAS THE BRISTOL FIGHTER.
○	○	2. THE COLD WAR CAME AFTER WORLD WAR TWO.
○	○	3. CHARLES ROLLS WAS THE SECOND PILOT TO QUALIFY IN BRITAIN.
○	○	4. AN AUTOGYRO CAN HOVER IN ONE PLACE.
○	○	5. ALCOCK AND BROWN CRASHED IN IRELAND.
○	○	6. THE JUPITER WAS A JET ENGINE.
○	○	7. SIR GEORGE WHITE WAS BORN IN 1910.
○	○	8. THE WINGS OF THE A400M ARE MADE FROM COMPOSITE MATERIAL.
○	○	9. ALL AEROPLANES WITH PISTON ENGINES HAVE PROPELLERS.
○	○	10. AMELIA EARHART WAS MARRIED IN 1974.

Back to the Drawing Board

To get a new type of aeroplane into the sky takes inspiration, imagination, hard work, trial and error, team-work, luck and lots of money, among other things. It could all start from a brand new idea that no one has ever thought of. More often, the idea improves or builds on something that has gone before. It might make an aeroplane that is bigger, safer, cheaper, more comfortable, stronger, faster, quieter or greener than others.

Saying something has to go 'back to the drawing board' means going back to the basic idea and starting again. That happens a lot in the development of something as big and complicated as an aeroplane. Here are pictures from the Bristol Aeroplane Company for aircraft that didn't get off the drawing board. Work like this is never wasted. Even if the actual aeroplane doesn't get into the sky, at least some of the ideas that got it onto paper can be used in the future. The engineers will also have a better idea of what will and what won't work when they try again. Both of these pictures are from the early 1960s. They show aircraft that can take off and land vertically or using a very short runway. One is in a remote jungle area where there are no runways at all. The other is on the roof of a building in New York. (ROLLS-ROYCE PLC)

Into the Future

Imagine it's 2030. An oil tanker is making its way across an ocean, unaware that it is being pursued by pirates. It's a dark, moonless night.

An unmanned surveillance aircraft is cruising through the skies, 20,000 metres above the water. It's been tirelessly and silently patrolling for the last few days, watching and waiting for something to happen. It's using an energy-efficient fuel-cell for power. It notices some suspicious activity on its radar and decides to investigate. The computerised control system switches from the fuel-cell to more powerful gas turbines so the aircraft can swoop down quickly and get a closer look.

The control system is also able to change the shape of the aircraft's wings. It's like an albatross when it's cruising, like a hawk when it's flying very fast. Unfortunately, as it dives it hits a real flock of birds and an engine is damaged. The sensors on the engine tell the control system the extent of the damage and the aircraft then decides how it can continue its mission. It sends a message to its operations centre back in Britain, ordering a replacement engine for when it returns to base. It also sends detailed pictures of the pirate boat to the nearest navy ship.

Artist's impression of new naval ship powered by Rolls-Royce engines.
(ROLLS-ROYCE PLC)

The operations centre makes sure a spare engine is ready for the surveillance aircraft so it can be quickly repaired and get back to work. The navy ship launches a super-fast unmanned combat aircraft from its deck which zooms into action and drops a bomb close to the pirates' boat to stop it chasing the tanker. The pirates had no idea the aircraft was coming as they couldn't see it with their infrared binoculars or pick it up with their radar equipment. That's because it uses very sophisticated stealth systems that make it hard to detect.

The combat aircraft returns to the navy ship, which has now also launched a new kind of helicopter that uses a combination of jet thrust and rotors to travel very fast. The 'compound' helicopter drops commandos to arrest the pirates.

People are already working on the technology that could make this future story possible. They are experimenting with advanced computerised control systems, unmanned aircraft, stealth systems and advanced helicopter engines. They are also working on more energy-efficient turbine engines that will use less fuel and produce less carbon dioxide than the ones being used today, and on materials for airframes that are more environmentally friendly.

Above is an artist's impression of Taranis. It is being developed to test ideas about how to build fast, unmanned military aircraft that can travel long distances and fly at low levels without being detected. Unmanned aircraft are useful for jobs that are dirty, dull or dangerous for humans. Piloting a bomber though heavily defended enemy territory is obviously dangerous work. Rolls-Royce is working on the engines that will power Taranis. It is expected to fly by the end of 2010. (BAE SYSTEMS)

At the top of the page opposite is a picture of an unmanned surveillance aircraft called Mantis. This made its first flight in 2009. The engines and surrounding pods were designed and built by Rolls-Royce. Engineers are developing unmanned surveillance aircraft that can stay in the air for very long periods of time. Being stuck up in the air for days on end, waiting for something to happen, is boring work for an experienced pilot, so it's better if a machine can do it. Surveillance aircraft don't usually need to be stealthy. Because they fly so high in the sky, keeping an eye on things over a large area, there is little risk of them being spotted or hit by missiles.

(BAE SYSTEMS)

On the right is a computer-generated picture of an open-rotor engine. Companies like Airbus are investigating how these types of engines might be used in future airliners. Open-rotors use less fuel and produce less carbon dioxide than modern turbofans. This is better for the environment. However, engineers are now having to solve one of the problems of this type of engine. They can be noisier than turbofans because there is no casing to absorb the sound of the blades turning.

(ROLLS-ROYCE PLC)

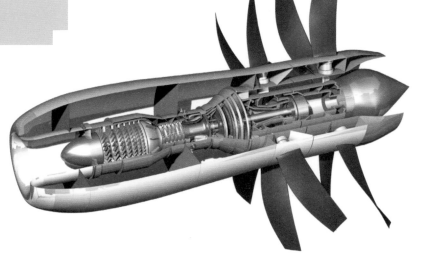

FIND OUT MORE

Websites with information and pictures about Bristol Aeroplane Company and many of the other companies mentioned in this book include:

BAC 100 2010: the official website for the Bristol Aeroplane Company birthday celebrations. It's got puzzles, games, fascinating facts, film clips, competitions and lots more.

www.bac2010.co.uk

Aviation Archive: a wonderful website chockfull of photos of West of England aircraft.

www.aviationarchive.org.uk

The Blenheim Society: celebrating a famous Bristol wartime aeroplane.

www.blenheimsociety.org.uk

Concorde: a tribute to the super sleek, supersonic aircraft.

www.concordesst.com

Speedbirds: another great website for Concorde fans.

www.speedbirds.com

Century of Flight: telling the story of flight from way back in 1783 to the present day.

www.century-of-flight.net

Aviation Ancestry: full of pictures of wonderful old aviation advertisements.

www.aviationancestry.com

Websites with activities linked to aviation include:

Alex's Paper Airplanes: we're big fans of Alex's paper aeroplane designs. The website includes video clips to help you follow the instructions. It also rates the aeroplanes as easy, medium and difficult so everyone should be able to find one they can make and fly.

www.paperairplanes.co.uk

Rolls-Royce plc: on this website there are activity sheets and interactive games. You'll have fun learning about engines, air resistance, fuel and other interesting things. Click on 'Activities for Primary Schools' and 'Activities for Secondary Schools' to find out more.

www.rolls-royce.com/cr/education/

NASA Kids' Club: NASA is the National Aeronautics and Space Administration in the USA. This website includes memory games and puzzles. Build your own dodecahedron decorated with aircraft pictures, help load Buzz Lightyear's shuttle and play I-Spy.

www.nasa.gov/audience/forkids/kidsclub/flash/index.html

Boeing Kids Page: Boeing is an American company that builds airliners and military aircraft. This page includes activity sheets you can print out. There are pictures to colour, mazes to explore and word games. There's also a section called 'Wonder of Flight' which explains how things fly and has information on different types of flying machines.

www.boeing.com/companyoffices/aboutus/kids/

Bristol Aero Collection Pages For Kids: this website has gliders to make, aircraft puzzles and other activities, links, and help and information for schools and youth groups wanting to visit the BAC museum at Kemble.

www.flyers.org.uk/BACEd/

Aviation places to visit in the UK include:

Bristol Aero Collection, Kemble Airfield, Gloucestershire
www.bristolaero.com

Concorde Visitors Centre, Filton, South Gloucestershire
www.concordeatfilton.org.uk

The Helicopter Museum, Weston-super-Mare
www.helicoptermuseum.co.uk

Imperial War Museum, Duxford
www.iwm.org.uk/duxford

National Museum of Flight, East Fortune, Scotland
www.nms.ac.uk/museumofflighthomepage.aspx

Royal Air Force Museum, Cosford
www.rafmuseum.org.uk/cosford/

Royal Air Force Museum, London
www.rafmuseum.org.uk/london/

Science Museum, London
www.sciencemuseum.org.uk

The Flight Zone at At-Bristol, Bristol Harbourside
www.at-bristol.org.uk

Shuttleworth Collection, Bedfordshire
www.shuttleworth.org

Fleet Air Arm Museum, Somerset
www.fleetairarm.com

Books to read:

There are lots of great books on aviation suitable for young and enthusiastic readers. Explore your local library and find out what's on the shelves. To start you off, here are a couple we used when we wrote this book:

Nick Arnold and Tony de Saulles (2004) *The Fearsome Fight for Flight* **Scholastic:** this is in the Horrible Science series. It's science with the squishy bits left in. Find out who put a parachute on a puppy, why scientists fire dead birds from cannon and what happened to the world's first flying sheep. With fantastic fact files, quirky quizzes and crazy cartoons, science has never been so horrible and so much fun.

Andrew Nahum (2003) *Flying Machine* **Dorling Kindersley:** this big book is full of wonderful pictures. Be an eyewitness to how humans first realised their dreams of taking flight and see the remarkable machines that have whisked us up, up, and away.

There are also some exciting novels for children about flight. One of our young friends recommends **W E John's** *Biggles and the Rescue Flight*. This is an action-packed story about two boys who run away from school during World War One, 'borrow' an aeroplane and fly off to France to find a missing brother. Another of our friends has recommended **Eoin Colfer's** *The Airman*. Fourteen-year-old Conor is framed for a terrible crime he didn't commit. He's thrown into a seaswept dungeon and branded a traitor. He must escape and clear his name. The only way out is to fly.

You can recommend your favourite books about flight by contacting us at BAC 100: bac100@btinternet.com

ACKNOWLEDGEMENTS

Lots of people helped to get this wonderful *Book of Aviation Wonder* together. We'd like to say a special personal 'Thank you' to:

Andrew Appleton, John Bradbrook, Linda Coode-Smith, Gareth Davies, David Hall, Patrick Hassell, John Heaven, Andrew Kelly, Jackie Sims, Barry Taylor, Sir George White Bt.

BAC 100 is a partnership project. We are grateful for the support of the companies and organisations listed opposite.

Beaufighter page reproduced from *The Bristol Story* (BCDP, 2008) by Eugene Byrne and Simon Gurr. All comic strips and puzzle pictures © Simon Gurr, 2010. All other text © Melanie Kelly, 2010. Illustrations on pages 31, 43, 54 and 83 © Vicky Washington, 2010.

In addition to those credited in the main text iStockphoto images were also used on the following pages: front and back covers, This book belongs to, Contents, 6, 15, 16, 28, 29, 30, 31, 38, 45, 48, 49, 53, 54, 73, 74, 75, 89, 94, 95.

'Sir George White – The Boxkite Baronet' uses material from *Tramlines to the Stars* by the current Sir George (Redcliffe Press).

Picture puzzle answers: Page 38: See illustration below. **Page 48:** See illustration below. **Page 73:** A Russia, B France, C Egypt, D India. **Page 89:** PROTEUS, DERWENT, PEGASUS, JUPITER, TURBINE, SQUEEZE.

Page 38:

Page 48:

Word puzzle answers: Page 38: Wilbur Wright, Henri Coanda, Charles Rolls, George Cayley, Maud Cook, Samuel Cody, George White, Orville Wright, Patrick Alexander, Vincenzo Lunardi. **Page 48:** 1D, 2F, 3A, 4G, 5I, 6J, 7C, 8B, 9H, 10E. **Page 73:** 1G, 2F, 3E, 4H, 5B, 6I, 7A, 8J, 9D, 10C. **Page 89:** 2, 3, 5, 8, 9.